27-96

Know buddy

294
RUG
2006

Religions and Religious Movements

JUDAISM

Other books in the Religions and
Religious Movements series:

Buddhism
Christianity
Confucianism
Hinduism
Islam

Religions and Religious Movements

JUDAISM

Adriane Ruggiero, Book Editor

Bruce Glassman, Vice President

Bonnie Szumski, Publisher, Series Editor

Helen Cothran, Managing Editor

GREENHAVEN PRESS
An imprint of Thomson Gale, a part of The Thomson Corporation

THOMSON

GALE

Detroit • New York • San Francisco • San Diego • New Haven, Conn.
Waterville, Maine • London • Munich

© 2006 Thomson Gale, a part of The Thomson Corporation.

Thomson and Star Logo are trademarks and Gale and Greenhaven Press are registered trademarks used herein under license.

For more information, contact
Greenhaven Press
27500 Drake Rd.
Farmington Hills, MI 48331-3535
Or you can visit our Internet site at http://www.gale.com

Cover credit: © Royalty-Free/CORBIS
Blackbirch Press, 117
Corel Corporation, 81, 103
UN Photo/John Isaac, 14

LIBRARY OF CONGRESS CATALOGING-IN-PUBLICATION DATA

Judaism / Adriane Ruggiero, book editor.
   p. cm. — (Religions and religious movements)
  Includes bibliographical references and index.
  ISBN 0-7377-2573-7 (lib. bdg. : alk. paper)
   1. Judaism. I. Ruggiero, Adriane. II. Series.
BM562.J83 2006
296—dc22   2005044167

Printed in the United States of America

$\mathscr{C}ontents$

a transcendent and unknowable God whose presence can be felt in the daily lives of ordinary humans.

Chapter 3: Rites, Rituals, and the Sacredness of Time

ing kosher," observant Jews impart spirituality to their everyday lives.

Chapter 4: Interpreting, Preserving, and Evolving

Chapter 5: Challenges Facing Jews Today

Orthodox, Conservative, and Reform—have formulated ways of confronting this challenge to Jewish identity.

Foreword

"Religion is not what is grasped by the brain, but a heart grasp."
—Mohandas Gandhi, 1956

The impulse toward religion—to move beyond the world as we know it and ponder the larger questions of why we are here, whether there is a God who directs our lives, and how we should live—seems as universally human as breathing.

Yet, although this impulse is universal, different religions and their adherents are often at odds due to conflicts that stem from their opposing belief systems. These conflicts can also occur because many people have only the most tentative understanding of religions other than their own. In a time when religion seems to be at the root of growing tensions around the world, its study seems particularly relevant.

We live in a religiously diverse world. And while the world's many religions have coexisted for millennia, only recently, with information shared so easily and travel to even the most remote regions made possible for larger numbers of people, has this fact been fully acknowledged. It is no longer possible to ignore other religions, regardless of whether one views these religions positively or negatively.

The study of religion has also changed a great deal in recent times. Just a few decades ago in the United States, few students were exposed to any religion other than Christianity. Today, the study of religion reflects the pluralism of American society and the world at large. Religion courses and even current events classes focus on non-Christian religions as well as the religious experiences of groups that have in the past been marginalized by traditional Christianity, such as women and racial minorities.

In fact, the study of religion has been integrated into many different types of classes and disciplines. Anthropology, psychology, sociology, history, philosophy, political science, economics, and other fields often include discussions about different nations' religions and beliefs.

The study of religion involves so many disciplines because, for many cultures, it is integrated into many different parts of life. This point is often highlighted when American companies conduct business deals in Middle Eastern countries and inadvertently offend a host country's religious constrictions, for example. On both a small scale, such as personal travel, and on a large scale, such as international trade and politics, an understanding of the world's religions has become essential.

The goals of the Religions and Religious Movements series are several. The first is to provide students a historical context for each of the world's religions. Each book focuses on one religion and explores, through primary and secondary sources, its fundamental belief system, religious works of importance, and prominent figures. By using articles from a variety of sources, each book provides students with different theological and historical contexts for the religion.

The second goal of the series is to explore the challenges that each religion faces today. All of these religions are experiencing challenges and changes—some theological, some political—that are forcing alterations in attitude and belief. By reading about these current dilemmas, students will come to understand that religions are not abstract concepts, but a vital part of peoples' lives.

The last and perhaps most important objective is to make students aware of the wide variety of religious beliefs, as well as the factors, common to all religions. Every religion attempts to puzzle out essential questions as well as provide a model for doing good in the world. By using the books in the Religions and Religious Movements series, students will find that people with divergent, closely held beliefs may learn to live together and work toward the same goals.

Introduction

Judaism's contribution to western religion is deep and complex. It was the first monotheistic religion, and is the basis for Christianity, the world's largest religion. Judaism is a complex marriage of history, ethnic identity, and lifestyle guidelines that inform everyday actions as well as spiritual decisions. For Orthodox Jews, who obey Judaism's tenants the most closely, the Torah, one of the Jewish holy texts, provides instruction on nearly every aspect of life. In fact, the Torah contains 613 commandments that instruct a person on everything from when and how to pray, what and how to eat, what to wear, and even how to care for livestock and pets. Indeed, philosopher Moses Mendelssohn once described Judaism as not a religion, but as law religionized.

Yet there is much diversity in the way Jews relate to the laws of Judaism. Some Jews believe that each law must be obeyed unquestioningly; other Jews believe it is appropriate to follow just some of the Bible's laws, and take the others as metaphor. Still other Jews may not practice the religion at all, or even believe in God—yet they still consider themselves Jews by birthright. Indeed, one of the most unique aspects of Judaism is that it joins those who view Judaism as a strict religious faith with those who view it as a secular identity.

Those who live their lives in strict accordance with the Bible's laws are known as Orthodox Jews. Many

Orthodox Jews live in tight-knit, distinctive communities that feature Hebrew newspapers, yeshivas (Jewish schools), and special religious stores that keep hours based on the Jewish calendar. In such communities, the customs and dress of the people clearly reflect Jewish law. For example, many Orthodox Jewish men wear a special garment under their clothing known as a tallis, which is a type of prayer shawl. Men wear this to help remind themselves of God's laws throughout the day, as they are ordered to do in Numbers 15:38. Orthodox men are also frequently seen wearing little boxes strapped to their heads and arms, near their heart. These are called tefillin and they contain scripture passages. Tefillin are worn in accordance with the commandment given in Deuteronomy 6:8, which instructs men to bind tefillin on the body in order to be mindful of God with all one's heart and mind. Yet another commandment, found in Leviticus 15:19–24, declares it is forbidden for men to touch a woman who is menstruating; for this reason, Orthodox men never hug or shake the hand of women they are not related to, for fear they may unwittingly make contact with a menstruating woman and break God's commandment.

Orthodox Jews believe that upholding Jewish law just as it is laid out in the Torah is the best way to practice their religion in accordance with God's wishes. Other interpretations of Judaism, however, have become popular with many Jews over the last two centuries. These Jews are less strict about following the laws of the Bible, but they retain certain elements of the culture that have meaning for them. This type of Judaism, known generally as Reform Judaism, flourished in the 1800s, when Jews began emigrating from their insulated communities to the cities of western Europe and the United States, which presented many new challenges. Many Jewish immigrants began to adjust their practice of Judaism in order fit into the predominantly Christian societies around them. Such tests of assimilation fueled the development of the Reform movement, which emphasized personal choice over strict adherence to law. Reform Judaism revolves around traditional associations with the Jewish home, including food, holiday celebrations, and other family rituals. In America, in particular, what defines large numbers of the Jewish community is a sense of cultural grounding in Jewish history and morals, rather than a sense of religious practice or spiritual belief.

A man instructs a young Jewish boy in the ritual donning of the tefillin, small boxes containing scripture passages.

Still other Jews may feel no spiritual connection to religion or even believe in God, but they regard Judaism as their ethnic or cultural identity and their birthright. Indeed, Jewishness, much like a nationality or an ethnicity, is inherited from one generation to the next regardless of one's belief about God: Jewish identity is officially passed from mother to child. Therefore, many Jews feel a sense of connection to the long lineage of Jews who came before them. Still other Jews feel an acute responsibility to retain elements of their Jewish identity as a way of paying homage to the previous generations who suffered in the Holocaust, or in the devastating pogroms that targeted Jews in Russia. Indeed, the trials of Jewish history give many modern Jews a sense that they must carry on the identity even if they eschew the religious aspects of the faith. British-Jewish novelist Anita Brookner once expressed this sense of obligation in the following way: "You can never betray the people who are dead, so you go on being a . . . Jew."

Such Jewish identity—that is, feeling culturally Jewish but not religiously Jewish—is often a source of tension in the wider Jewish community. Orthodox Jews, for example, tend to view these Jews as illegitimate. They object to Reform Jews picking and choosing a few pleasant associations with the culture and still considering themselves Jewish. Some Orthodox Jews actually prefer the label "Torah-true," because they feel they are the only Jews upholding Jewish law. In return, many non-Orthodox Jews look with equal negativity upon the Orthodox, whom they see as consumed with practicing the religion to the letter, at times to the exclusion of the modern world around them. Creating personal expressions of Jewishness is very meaningful for many non-Orthodox Jews, who do not believe that ritual for the sake of ritual is as valuable as making informed choices about their beliefs.

Today, the different movements and sects of Judaism make it a religion with division, yet most Jews retain a sense of belonging to one people with one shared destiny set in motion thousands of years ago. They are able to do so because being Jewish is at once being part of both a religious faith and an ethnic culture. As Rabbi Stephen M. Wylen has observed: "Culture, customs, ethics, sense of self—these are all part of Judaism as much as the faith and the rituals of the Jewish religion."[1] The viewpoints presented in *Religions and Religious Movements: Judaism* explore the ancient history, religious beliefs, sacred rituals, cultural associations, and modern debates of the spiritual faith and ethnic identity that is Judaism.

Note

1. Stephen M. Wylen, *Settings of Silver: An Introduction to Judaism.* New York: Paulist Press, 1989, p. 3.

CHAPTER 1

A People, a Place, a Faith

What Is Judaism?

by Hayim Halevy Donin

Judaism is a broad term that encompasses the civilization of the Jewish people, their faith as practiced over thousands of years of history, and the rituals and writings that set them apart from other communities of believers. The core of Judaism is its pronouncement of the existence of one God and his choice of the Jews as a chosen people who will establish an example for all nations. These are some of the concepts described in the following selection from *To Be a Jew* by Rabbi Hayim Halevy Donin, a teacher and interpreter of Jewish law. Many Jews regard this work as a classic guide for the understanding and daily practice of Judaism.

Donin's audience is made up of non-Jews, converts to Judaism, and Jews who wish to learn about their faith. He describes the origin of terms such as *Hebrew*, *Israelite*, *Jew*, and *Judah* and then focuses on the concepts of Jewish uniqueness and inclusivity. Donin makes the point that while their beliefs made them separate and distinct from other peoples, Jews through four thousand years of history have interacted with other cultures. As a civilization they have been both remarkably continuous and adaptable, despite persecution and near annihilation. Above all, observant Jews are guided by their belief that they are servants of God and must do his bidding in all things.

Hayim Halevy Donin, Rabbi, *To Be a Jew: A Guide to Jewish Observance in Contemporary Life*. New York: Basic Books, 1972. Copyright © 1972 by Rabbi Hayim Halevy Donin. Reprinted by permission of Basic Books, a member of Perseus Books, LLC.

Hayim Halevy Donin was rabbi of Congregation B'nai David in Southfield, Michigan, and was also a professor of Jewish studies at the University of Detroit. He died in 1982. Donin's other works include *To Pray as a Jew* and *To Raise a Jewish Child.*

The terms *Hebrew, Israelite,* and *Jew* have historically been used synonymously and interchangeably. The Bible refers to Abraham as Ibri (Hebrew), probably because he migrated from the other side (east) of the Euphrates River [a major river of the Middle East; flows through Turkey, Syria, and Iraq] and Ibri means "from the other side." Israel was the alternate name of Jacob, the grandson of Abraham. Hence his twelve sons and their descendants became known as the children of Israel, or the Israelite Nation or People. Jew is derived from Judah, the son of Israel, the most prominent of the Twelve Tribes. This became the prevalent name for the entire people when the Judeans from the Kingdom of Judea survived the downfall of the Northern Kingdom of Israel in 722 B.C. when Ten Tribes were led into captivity. Thus today, the people are called Jewish, their faith Judaism, their language Hebrew, and their land Israel.

The Family of Believers

This people, Israel, started life as one family tracing its antecedents back to Abraham, the Hebrew who lived approximately 3800 years ago. The monotheistic [meaning "belief in one God"] faith firmly held by Abraham, and the "Covenant with God" entered into by him and reaffirmed by his descendants, identified this family as the adherents of a special faith. The family did not claim exclusive rights to this faith, but on the contrary, were eager to attract others to it. As this God-intoxicated family and those who joined them in faith grew in number, accepting the Torah [the Jewish Law] as their Divine Constitution, taking possession of the land promised to them by the Master of the universe, they assumed the characteristics of a nation, a people speaking a common language, living within a specified geographic area, sharing common memories and a common destiny, and exercising the attributes of national sovereignty.

On the basis of their origin, Jews everywhere have regarded themselves as members of a family, an expanded family to be sure, and oftimes a far-flung family, but a family nevertheless. Membership in this family derives from the mother. The child of any Jewish woman is thus considered to be a member of the family. But membership in the family has never been limited by birth. It has always been open to all, and those who share the faith of this family may be "adopted" into it. Thus, the convert to Judaism not only becomes a partner in faith with the children of Israel, but through faith, the proselyte [convert] himself becomes one of the children of Israel, sharing fully in its heritage and its privileges and assuming its burdens and tribulations. In accepting the Jewish faith, the proselyte thus joins the Jewish people or nation. In accepting the religious duties of the present, and in assuming the spiritual mission of the future, he also ties himself to the collective past.

Although the natural tendency for any family is to be exclusive and to look inward, this particular family was never exclusive. In times of persecution it was sometimes forced to withdraw in self-defense, but generally it looked outward and reached out to the world at large. When the central sanctuary in Jerusalem was built, Jews saw it as a "House of Prayer for all peoples" (Isaiah 56:7, see also I Kings 8:41–43).

In the very emphasis upon the particular, this singular family reflected the noblest form of universalism. The universalism that permeates the faith of Israel is reflected not only in its theological formulations and in its visions of the future, but in the very composition of its people. This seemingly "exclusive" people includes those whose skins range from the lightest to the darkest in colors, and within it a broad range of cultural diversity is represented. Yet despite the diversity that exists among them and the multitude of languages they speak, Jews regard themselves as related, as true brethren stemming from a common Semitic [meaning, of or related to the language family that includes Hebrew, Aramaic, and Arabic] family. Although it is religion which unites them and it is only on the basis of religion that newcomers are admitted into fellowship, this feeling of kinship is very strong—and the mystery deepens when we realize that even Jews who rebel against the faith and discard its religious beliefs and practices are still regarded as Jews, and generally themselves still feel the bonds of kinship.

This sense of kinship felt by the Jewish people may be more of a "mystical" experience than a rationally definable one. Perhaps that is one of the reasons why Jews have never quite been able to fit into the convenient categories used by historians or sociologists to define nations, races, religions, and other social groupings. Except for the fact that the Jews obviously do not constitute a race (for race is a biological designation), the Jews are *not just* a religious faith, even though they are that; and they are *not just* a nation, even though they are that too, according to definitions of the term "nation." The problem is usually resolved by using the term "people" instead of either "faith" or "nation."

This difficulty in categorizing the Jewish people may well be part of their uniqueness. It is a uniqueness which according to the believer was given its permanent stamp by the Divine command, "You shall be to Me a kingdom of priests and a holy nation" (Exodus 19:6). . . .

A History of Contributing

Although a small people, separate and distinct, Israel has nevertheless not been a withdrawn people. Though standing alone, it has not stood aside. Jewish history is interlaced with that of every other nation and empire. "Jews . . . have witnessed and taken part in more of the human career, they have recorded more of it, shaped more of it, originated and developed more of it, above all, suffered more of it, than any other people," wrote Ernest van den Haag. The history of the Jews has been a history of interaction with the rest of the world— although Western scholars reared in a Christian-dominated society have tended to perceive only myopically the role of the Jew and of Judaism in that history, and to treat condescendingly anything that related to Jews or to Judaism. Textbooks of history, sociology or philosophy rarely have anything significant to say about the Jewish people or Jewish thought after the beginning of the Christian era. The bias against Judaism and the Jews that was reflected for so long in the texts and the curricula of the Christian universities was bequeathed to the secular academic world even after theological influence waned and the institutions became secular. Even Jews who entered this academic milieu were subtly influenced by the existing bias and unquestioningly accepted it themselves. Generally ignorant of their own history and philosophy, they fell sway to the notion that serious Jewish thought beyond the Biblical period either did not exist or did not merit the concern of serious scholarship.

Though denied, despised, rejected, persecuted, confined, and restricted through history, Jews and Judaism, the people itself and its sacred books, have nonetheless often set in motion forces that marked major revolutionary changes and advances in Western religions, in the natural and medical sciences, and in social philosophies. The contributions by individual Jews in every field of creative endeavor, in the advancement of human knowledge, in the elimination of suffering, in the development of commerce, have filled volumes. Judaism's traditional emphasis on social justice through social action has had a noticeable effect in contemporary times.

For a people who have always been numerically insignificant, "the fewest of all the nations," *ha-m'at at mikol ha-amim* to use the words of the Torah, to have compiled such a record of achievements, and to have been on the scene of world history for so long while surviving all attempts to assimilate it and even to annihilate it, *something* more must be involved than the capacities of the people themselves.

"You Did God Choose"

The devout Jew looks upon that "something more" as a fulfillment of Divine prophecy that "through you and your descendants will all the families of the earth be blessed" (Genesis 28:14), and as a vindication of Israel's

Covenant with God: "For you are a holy people unto the Lord your God, and you did God choose to be unto Him a treasured people from among all the peoples upon the face of the earth" (Deut. 14:2). The devout Jew accepts the status with humility and thanksgiving, seeing it as a yoke and a burden as well as a distinction. He sees himself as a servant of the Lord, ready to do His bidding at all times. Serving the Lord takes many forms: spending one's life studying Torah, faithfully observing the ritual and ethical commandments, struggling for justice and righteousness in society. The learned and observant Jew ignores none of the ways.

Whatever the believing Jew may find himself doing in fulfillment of that role, and whatever apparent "smallness" or "insignificance" his existence may appear to have, for him there is cosmic significance and purpose in doing the bidding of the Lord.

The skeptical Jew, on the other hand, who does not at all see himself as a servant of the Lord, is embarrassed by any reference to Israel's enjoyment of Divine favor or any notion of a special national mission. Such talk even on the part of non-Jews tends to embarrass him, and he is eager to repudiate all such notions. But his attempts at repudiating the meaning of Jewish history are invariably contradicted by history itself, which does not permit Jews to become "like all the other nations," to become merely another national entity among nations.

We believe that the nations and peoples of the world have their Divine purposes and their assigned roles to fulfill, too, for God is the God of all the world, not just of Jewry. And we see our divinely ordained assignment as involving a unique role, one to which history itself bears witness. It implies a special purpose in life, a reason for our existence. That purpose is not to make Jews of all the world, but to bring the peoples of the world, whatever their distinctive beliefs may be, to an acknowledgment of the sovereignty of God and to an acceptance of the basic values revealed to us by that God. It is to serve as a means by which blessing will be brought to "all the families of the earth" (Genesis 12:3).

It is this mission which underlies for Jews the coming of the day "when the world shall be perfected under the reign of the Almighty, and all mankind will call upon Thy name." It is only in these terms, supernatural though they be, that any plausible explanation can be offered for Israel's ability to survive against the many obstacles and threats to its very existence, and its success in penetrating the thought of most nations. It is in these terms that we discover meaning even in Israel's historical suffering and dispersion [scattering] as in its achievements, its strengths, and its restoration to Zion [the Promised Land in which God dwells among his chosen people].

The Ancient Hebrews: A Historian's View

by Norman F. Cantor

According to the late historian Norman F. Cantor, the ancient Hebrews may have been a people of the eastern
Mediterranean who conquered the land of Canaan and
settled there. Or they may have been a subgroup of the
Canaanites themselves. What made them unique was
their belief that God (whom they called Yahweh or Jehovah) had chosen them as his own people. This great gift
was accompanied by great obligations, something which
the Hebrews could not disown. The Jewish covenant, or
agreement, with God was, in Cantor's words, "their burden and their glory." It is also this covenant, not great art
or monuments, that comprises the Jews' unique contribution to civilization.

In the following selection Cantor describes the ancient
history of the Hebrews; their kings Saul, David, and
Solomon; and especially the prophets, individuals who
exhorted the Hebrews to remain inwardly *and* outwardly
true to the covenant. As a historian living in the twentieth century, Cantor chooses to call the Hebrew prophets
"progressives," reformers who demanded morality and
social justice and the pure worship of Yahweh. The author's primary focus is on the concept of the Jews'
covenant with God. In Cantor's words, it is this covenant

that is "the foundation myth of Jewish history."

Canadian-born, Cantor was a leading scholar of medieval history and the author of the textbook *The Civilization of the Middle Ages* and the historical study *In the Wake of the Plague.* He died in 2004 at age seventy-four. Cantor taught at Columbia University, Brandeis, SUNY Binghamton, and the University of Illinois at Chicago. Before his retirement Cantor was dean of the College of Arts and Sciences at New York University.

Whether the Israelites of the early first millennium B.C. were a nomadic people who came out of the southern desert to overrun the urbanized Canaanites along the eastern littoral [shore] of the Mediterranean, or whether they were originally a religious or social subgroup among the Canaanites themselves, they became bound together in a loose political confederation. More important they had a religious identity—their devotion to their god Yahweh (YHWH, Jehovah) and the belief they were bound to him by a covenant (B'rit).

Whatever had been the origin of these people called Israel, they were now a people collectively and identifiably called by God. Yahweh would protect the tribes of Israel, and in return they must obey certain religious commands set down by him. The Jews also cultivated a memory (however invented) of the captivity of some of their tribes in Egypt and their rescue from Egypt by Yahweh through the leadership of Moses. Despite a tendency to confuse Yahweh with local gods and to worship according to the forms practiced by the Canaanites, these traditions were assiduously cultivated.

The covenant was not a negotiated contract—the Jews

had not entered voluntarily into a compact with Yahweh, nor could they withdraw from their obligations to God. Of his own inscrutable will, Yahweh had chosen this obscure people as his own. . . .

The Covenant Idea

The covenant idea was that God had given to the fathers of the tribe—Abraham, Isaac, and Jacob—the land of Canaan as their own land, and when the Jews were slaves of Pharaoh in Egypt, he had sent Moses to lead them out of captivity and back to the Promised Land. Yahweh had also imposed on his people his ethical norms and religious commandments, beginning with the tablets accorded Moses on Mount Sinai. The Jews had no choice but to maintain God's covenant—this was their burden and their glory.

The power and meaning of the covenant is adumbrated [foreshadowed] early in the Bible in the story of Abraham's willingness to sacrifice his son Isaac at God's command. Of course, divine intervention precludes this killing of the child, but that Abraham was willing to perform this heinous ritual at God's command is held to be meritorious and worthy of immense reward. The covenant has been upheld, even to the point of death, and Yahweh is immensely pleased:

> By Myself I swear, the Lord declares: Because you have done this and have not withheld your son, your favored one, I will bestow My blessings upon you and make your descendants as numerous as the stars of heaven and the sand on the seashore: And your descendants shall seize the gates of their foes. All the nations shall bless themselves by your descendants, because you have obeyed My command.

The story of the sacrifice of Isaac had a profound message for the Hebrew mind down through the centuries.

In biblical history, the people complained often enough and aroused God's wrath frequently enough by violating the covenant, even to the point of worshipping idols and false gods. But the people had been called, and they could not repudiate the covenant. The prescribed circumcision of all Jewish males memorialized the eternity of the covenant. The benign Sabbath symbolized the covenant's continuing humane value in Jewish life.

In this land of Canaan that God gave to Abraham, his seed would prosper and multiply. Abraham would be "the father of a multitude of nations." Canaan would be "an everlasting holding" of the people of the covenant:

> I am God Almighty. Live always in my presence and be perfect, so that I may put my covenant between me and you. . . . I am setting up my covenant between me and you and your descendants after you as an eternal covenant, to be your God and the God of your descendants. And I am giving you and your descendants after you the land where you are now aliens, the whole of the land of Canaan as an eternal possession, and I will be God to them. . . . You shall circumcise the flesh of your foreskin, and this shall be the sign of the covenant between me and you.

These words of Yahweh to Abraham in the Book of Genesis are the foundation myth of Jewish history, the idea out of which the sacred chain of self-imposed collective Jewish destiny was forged.

This theme is reinforced in the Book of Exodus by God's message to the people of Israel assembled at the foot of Mount Sinai:

> And now, if you hear my voice and observe my covenant, you shall be my possession before all the

peoples; for the whole earth is mine. You shall become to me a kingdom of priests and a holy people.

The covenant idea is the polar opposite of democracy, multiculturalism, and ethnic equality. It is in-
tensely elitist. It singles out the people of Israel and
raises them uniquely above all other people as a holy
community of priests designated to witness God's word
in the world, as summarized in the Decalogue, the Ten
Commandments that Moses received from Yahweh on
Mount Sinai:

> I am the Lord your God.
> You shall have no other gods besides me.
> You shall not make for yourselves an image of God.
> You shall not take the name of the Lord your God
>   in vain.
> Remember the sabbath day to keep it holy.
> Honor your father and mother.
> You shall not kill.
> You shall not commit adultery.
> You shall not steal.
> You shall not bear false witness against your
>   neighbor.
> You shall not covet your neighbor's house.
> You shall not covet your neighbor's wife . . . or
>   anything that is your neighbor's.

Early Kings

Bound together by these beliefs and moral law, the Jewish tribes overcame the power of hostile Canaanites, we
are told. In the tenth century B.C. the tribes of Israel,
faced with a great threat from the Philistines, united
into one kingdom. David, later remembered as their
greatest king, was able to defeat the enemies of Israel
and to establish a hegemony [dominance] in the land.
He captured the hill city of Jerusalem and made it the

capital of his empire. In the reign following David's, his son, rich and mighty Solomon, built the Temple, which was to become the center of religious observance in Israel. The rise of David's monarchy (tenth century B.C.) can be perceived from circumstantial biblical accounts reinforced by meager archaeological data.

The emergence of kingship among the Israelites in the ninth century B.C. was the consequence of the invasion of Canaan from the Mediterranean side by a sea people, the Philistines, who possessed superior iron weapons. The Philistine center was along the southern coast in places like Ashdod and Ashqelon. In response to this threat, the Hebrews could no longer rely on the leadership of "judges," ad hoc military leaders (some of them peculiarly women, perhaps reflecting, as feminists claim, an earlier matriarchal society). The Hebrews needed the continuity and strength of a united monarchy.

The first such king, Saul, was given divine sanction for his rule over the people by the ceremony of anointment, wherein the high priest Samuel poured holy oil on Saul's head. Even though Saul came from the smallest of the Hebrew tribes, his anointment to the kingship and some early success against the Philistines won him popularity and loyalty. The ambitious leader of a powerful mercenary band, David, from the largest of the tribes, Judah, would not raise his hand against anointed Saul and try to overthrow him, despite increasing tension between the two power brokers.

When Saul and his sons fell fighting against the Philistines, David took the kingship, defeated the Philistines (from whom the Jews learned iron-making and to whom they gave their alphabet), and set up his capital in the newly conquered citadel of Jerusalem, on the high arid inland plateau. A convenient court seer proclaimed the durability of David's line despite the king's boisterous

Moses: Leader, Lawgiver, and Prophet

Moses, born during the reign of the Egyptian pharaoh Rameses II (1304 B.C.–1237 B.C.), is the most significant person in the emergence of Judaism. Raised as a prince in the household of the pharaoh, he led the Israelites out of Egypt into the Promised Land. The late Israeli statesman Abba Eban wrote the following profile of Moses in his book Heritage: Civilization and the Jews.

Moses was born and bred into Egyptian life and tradition. Yet he was of Hebrew ancestry, and the persecution of his kinsmen moved him to ardent and creative anger. Out of his indignation there would emerge events and new understandings, unique for his time . . . and valid for all generations. . . .

In the Bible, the revolt of the Hebrews begins with an isolated act of indignation—and compassion.

> And it came to pass in those days, when Moses was grown, that he went out unto his brethren, and looked on their burdens: and he spied an Egyptian smiting an Hebrew, one of his brethren.
> And he looked this way and that way, and when he saw that there was no man, he slew the Egyptian, and hid him in the sand.
>
> (Exodus 2:11–12)

But this act of righteous indignation, supposedly executed in secret, does not remain secret very long. Moses has been sexual behavior. An elaborate system of cisterns and wells, now again visible after recent archaeological discovery, provided water to the new Jewish citadel.

observed, and when report of his action reaches Pharaoh, Moses is forced to flee. In exile in the land of the Midianites, in the wilderness of Sinai, Moses marries Zipporah, the daughter of a Midianite priest. It is in Sinai, at Horeb, that Moses first hears the voice of God, coming from a bush that burns "with fire" but that the fire does not consume:

> Now therefore, behold, the cry of the children of Israel is come unto me: and I have also seen the oppression wherewith the Egyptians oppress them.
>
> Come now therefore, and I will send thee unto Pharaoh, that thou mayest bring forth my people the children of Israel out of Egypt.
>
> (Exodus 3:9–10)

In speaking of God, Moses was capable of an unprecedented exercise in abstraction. He could envisage a God above nature, a God immune from human passion and natural vicissitudes.

Uniting the Israelites in the worship of a single God, Moses managed, without physical authority or sanction at his command, to organize the straggling seminomad tribes for concerted revolt and to lead them out of their Egyptian birthplace in an Exodus from slavery to freedom.

Abba Eban, *Heritage: Civilization and the Jews.* New York: Summit, 1984, pp. 24–26.

Solomon, the son produced by the most scandalous of David's numerous unions, ruled temporarily an imperial territory larger than Israel itself. Solomon generated high-glitz court glamour, and he too enjoyed a multitude of wives and concubines. He imposed heavy taxation on the people to build the Temple in Jerusalem. Here was centralized the sacrifice of animals to Yahweh. And the Temple priesthood came to play a dominant role in religious life.

Nothing in the story of David and Solomon, told with elaborate detail in the Bible, distinguishes them from any other minor dynasty of the ancient Near East—except the commitment to Yahweh and the covenant, even though Solomon had a relish for Gentile [non-Jewish] women.

The period of a united empire was brief. After Solomon's death in 931 B.C. the empire disintegrated into two kingdoms—Israel in the north and Judah in the south, reflecting long-standing separatist tendencies. Neither kingdom was able to retain its independence for long. The two kingdoms were so placed between Egypt and the Mesopotamian empires that they were frequently the scene of recurrent battles between the contending great powers. Finally, Assyria extended its predominance from Mesopotamia and reduced the two Jewish kingdoms to a state of vassalage.

During the period that Israel and Judah were menaced by the great powers, Jewish religious practices and beliefs changed—partly in response to the foreign threat and partly in reaction to conditions within Israel itself. Along with the worship of Yahweh, there had also been, from the tenth until the eighth century B.C., worship at other shrines. Intermarriage with foreigners was frequent, and because Yahweh was worshipped at local shrines, there was a tendency to fuse him with the gods of the locality. There was another significant social change: In contrast to the conditions of relative social and economic equality that had prevailed in primitive tribal times, the community was becoming increasingly separated into rich and poor. The characteristic Near Eastern social conflict of landlord against peasant, town against country, royalty and priesthood against commoner prevailed.

The Prophets: Truth-Speakers

The prophetic movement of the eighth to the sixth century B.C. attributed the impending misfortunes of Israel to its forsaking of the covenant with Yahweh. The prophets were visionaries and rigorous moralists who made public pronouncements communicating Yahweh's current message to the people of the covenant. The prophets did not advocate simply a return to the practices and way of life of earlier times. They were progressives who demanded fulfillment of morality and social justice and the pure worship of Yahweh. To save the nation, it would be necessary to purify national life and reform society.

Some of the prophets were associated with the Temple. Some represented political factions within the nation. Yet they were always individuals whose personal experiences led them to believe that they were chosen by Yahweh to speak to the nation on his behalf. Often they experienced communication with Yahweh through ecstatic visions, and they felt compelled to convey his message to the nation regardless of its reception or the consequences. Unfortunately, the writings of the major prophets in the Hebrew Bible were much edited in later centuries, and texts do not well disclose the individual personalities of most of the prophets.

The prophets spoke out to the Jews in the mid-eighth century B.C. with a common message. In the northern kingdom of Israel, two prophets, Amos and Hosea, foretold the destruction of Israel. Amos asserted that the demands of Yahweh were moral and spiritual, spoke against the oppression of the poor by the rich, and attacked the ritualistic practices of Israel. His contemporary, Hosea, explicitly named the Assyrians as the instrument by which Yahweh would destroy Israel if it did not repent. In the kingdom of Judah to the south, the warnings and demands of Amos and Hosea were echoed by the prophet Isaiah, who identified the sin of Israel as its rebellion against Yahweh, and by Micah, who, like Amos, called for an end to chronic social grievances.

The prophets did more than attack the syncretic blending of the Hebrew faith with other cults and excessive attention to ritualistic externals. They insisted that Yahweh was the one and only God and that obedience to Him and fulfillment of His ethical demands was the only possible course for the salvation of the Jewish nation. Eventually their calls for reform profoundly influenced the official—priestly and royal—position that they sometimes criticized. The oppositional character of prophecy was steadily moderated into one of cooperation with the ruling group.

The destruction of the northern kingdom of Israel at the hands of the Assyrians under Sargon II in 721 B.C. made more insistent the prophets' religious demands in the surviving Judean kingdom in the south.

The Hebrew word for prophet is *nabi*, one who calls or is called. A prophet in ancient Judaism is not someone who predicts the future, although the Hebrew prophets did plenty of that. It is rather someone called by God to proclaim or communicate his word. Therefore the prophets are God's chosen successors to Abraham and Moses as truth-speakers of divine intelligence. . . .

The most interesting text in this regard is in the Book of Isaiah, where God seems to look askance upon fasting in comparison with activist social justice:

> Is such a fast I desire a day for men to starve their bodies? Is it bowing the head like a bulrush and lying in sackcloth and ashes? . . .
>
> No, unlock fetters of wickedness, and untie the cords of the yoke, to let the oppressed go free. . . .

A Religion of Command and Moral Commitment

Today the almost universal view among Jewish scholars is that Isaiah is not placing justice over a code of prescribed religious praxis [practice] but instead is saying that the latter must be fulfilled by the spirit and sensibility of the former. A behavioral code without intense moral consciousness is not the Jewish way. Law fulfilled by justice is the Jewish way.

Already in ancient times, this section of Isaiah was read aloud to the congregation on the Day of Atonement [one of the holiest days in the Jewish calendar] to remind the community that the Law must be fulfilled inwardly as well as outwardly. This is the prophetic message, so that even if the prophets may have started out as critics of the priesthood, the two religious ways rapidly coalesced. Today this is the consensus view of the prophets among Jewish biblical scholars.

The essence of biblical Judaism is the blending of a legalistic with a prophetic tradition—a religion of command with a religion of moral commitment. In the Book of Deuteronomy, drawn up in its present version in the seventh century B.C., after the era of the great prophets, this blending of law and prophecy, command and commitment, takes the definitive form of God saying: "I have put before you life and death, blessing and curse. Choose life . . . by loving the Lord your God, heeding His commands and holding fast to Him."

The prophet Isaiah blends the covenant ideas with Israel's designated role in spreading God's message of justice and love to the whole world:

> This is My servant, whom I uphold, my chosen one, in whom I delight. He shall teach the true way to the nations. . . .
>
> He shall not grow dim or be bruised till he has established the true way on earth. . . .
>
> I the Lord, in My grace, have summoned you, and I have grasped you by the hand. I created you and appointed you a covenant people, a light of nations.

The Bible as Divine Revelation

by F.E. Peters

Judaism, Christianity, and Islam are all scriptural religions in that they affirm the existence of God's revelation in written form. For Jews, God's word is contained in the Bible, a work which consists of several books: Torah, Prophets, and Writings. For Christians, it is revealed in both the Old Testament of the Jewish Bible and the story of Jesus's life and deeds as told in the New Testament. For Muslims, it is revealed in the Koran as told to the prophet Muhammad. Because of the existence of these books or scriptures, Jews, Christians, and Muslims are identified as "people of the book," the term applied to them by Muslims.

F.E. Peters, the author of the following selection, is a professor of Middle Eastern studies, history, and religion at New York University. His topic in this selection is the common foundations of the world's three monotheistic religions. Each faith worships one God who happens to be the same God though called by different names: Yahweh by the Jews, God the Father by Christians, and Allah by Muslims. For Jews, God's revelation is contained in the Torah and also in the other books of the Bible: Prophets and Writings. As described by Peters, the Hebrew Bible is a "composite blend of religious myth, historical narrative, legal enactments, prophetic admonitions, cautionary tales, and poetry composed over a long span of time." Peters points out that all three sibling faiths regard their sacred book as complete, final, and authoritative.

F.E. Peters is the author of several works on religion, including *The Monotheists: Jews, Christians, and Muslims in Conflict and Competition* and *Islam: A Guide for Jews and Christians.*

Judaism, Christianity, and Islam are all scriptural religions, that is, they affirm the existence of a divine revelation in written form. "The Sacred Writings," "The Scripture" or "The Book" are practically interchangeable terms among the three, and their adherents can all be identified as "People of the Book," as the Muslims in fact call them. More, these revelations from on high represent God's intervention in history; and, indeed, the same God: the Jews' Yahweh, the Christians' God the Father who is in Heaven, and the Muslims' Allah is one and the same deity, with the same history, the same attributes and, in fact, the same name.

God's Revelation

The three Scriptures show marked differences, however. In the Jewish—and Muslim—view, God gave and Moses [Hebrew lawgiver and prophet] wrote down a distinct and discrete [consisting of distinct parts] multipart book, the Law or Torah. But though the Torah holds pride of place in Jewish revelational history, God's direct interventions were in one manner or another continuous between Moses and Ezra [Hebrew priest and scribe; key figure in the book of Ezra] and thus the Jewish Bible is a collective work that includes, under the three headings of Law, Prophets, and the miscellany called Writings, all of God's revelation to His people.

This was certainly the Jewish view in Jesus' day, and there is no reason to think that Jesus regarded Scripture any differently. He in turn produced no new Writings or Book of his own, and so Christian "Scripture" is formally quite different from what the Jews thought of as such. The Gospels are accounts of Jesus' words and deeds set down, in approximately a biographical framework, by his followers. In the eyes of Christians, Jesus did not bring a Scripture; he was himself, in his person and message, a revelation, the "Good News." His life and sacrificial death sealed a "New Covenant" that God concluded with His people, and so the Gospels and the accounts of the deeds and thoughts of the early Christian community recorded in the Acts of the Apostles and the letters of various of Jesus' followers came to be regarded by Christians as a New Testament to be set down next to the Old, that recorded and commemorated in the Jewish Bible.

Muhammad may have had only an imperfect understanding of this somewhat complex process. Though he commonly refers to the Jewish revelation as "Tawrah." the Prophet of Islam was certainly aware that there were other Jewish prophets, and so possibly revelations, after Moses. But he never mentions a New Testament; his sole references are to "the gospel," in Arabic *injil*, and he seems to have thought of it as a sacred book that Jesus had brought or written, much as Moses had the Torah.

Muhammad had a strong sense of the prophetic

Bible Translation: An Overview

Bible translation began about 2,200 years ago, in the third century B.C., as the large Jewish population of Alexandria, Egypt, came under the influence of Hellenism. When the Greek language replaced Hebrew and Aramaic as their vernacular, and the Torah in its Hebrew original was no longer commonly understood, a translation into Greek was made for the Jewish community of Alexandria. This translation came to be known as the Septuagint, Latin for "seventy," because of the legend that the committee of translators numbered seventy-two, six elders from each of the twelve tribes of Israel.

In the last few centuries B.C., the Jews who lived to the north and east of Judea also found the Hebrew Bible difficult to understand, for their spoken language had become largely Aramaic. Translations into Aramaic, first of the Torah and then of the rest of the Bible, became known as the Targums.

The Septuagint and the Targums are not only the oldest translations of the Bible but also the most influential. Down to our own day, virtually every Christian translation has followed the methods of the Jewish translators who created the Septuagint, and generally followed their renderings of the Hebrew as well. The Christian translators also were influenced by the interpretation of the Hebrew text set forth in the Targums (much of it in oral form at the time) and by the writings of the Jewish philosopher-interpreter Philo of Alexandria (died about A.D. 45). . . .

With the growth of Christianity in the first century, the Church adopted the Septuagint as its Bible, and the Septuagint was translated into the languages of the various Christian communities. As Greek began to give way to Latin in the Roman Empire, it was only a matter of time before a Latin translation of Scripture became the recognized Bible of the Church. The Church father Jerome (c. 340–420) produced the official Latin version. Drawing on Jewish tradition and consulting Jewish teachers, he achieved what came to be known as the Vulgate, the Bible in the language of the common people. The Vulgate, the Bible of European Christianity until the Reformation, is clearly the most significant Bible translation after the Septuagint.

With the rise of Protestantism in Europe, scholars within this movement set themselves the task of making the Bible available in the various vernaculars of the time. By 1526 the first parts of the two notable translations began to appear: Martin Luther's in German and William Tyndale's in English. The latter, by way of several subsequent revisions, became the King James Version of 1611. The more modern English versions—such as *The Holy Scriptures* by the American rabbi Isaac Leeser (1855), the (British) Revised Version (1881–1885), the American Standard Version (1901), the Jewish Publication Society's *The Holy Scriptures* (1917), and the (American) Revised Standard Version (1952)—made extensive use of the King James.

Jewish Publication Society, *Tanakh: A New Translation of the Holy Scriptures According to the Traditional Hebrew Text*. Philadelphia: Jewish Publication Society, 1985, pp. xv–xvi.

calling and of the line of prophets that had created the Judeo-Christian tradition, and after some brief initial hesitation, he placed himself firmly within that line. He too was a prophet, and now in these latter times, when His earlier revelations had become distorted at the willful and perverse hands of the Jews and Christians. God had given to him, no less than to Moses and Jesus, a revealed Book. Or so it was in its final, codified version. What God Himself had instructed Muhammad to call The Recitation, in Arabic *al-Qur'an*, was in fact a series of messages delivered to Muhammad by the Angel Gabriel over a period of twenty-two years. Each part was already identified as Scripture during the Prophet's lifetime, and the Book was finally closed only with Muhammad's death.

Three Sacred Books

Thus there came into being three Sacred Books, each in some sense the Word of God; each regarded as a complete, final, and authoritative statement regulating the role and conduct of men vis-à-vis their Creator; and each a birthright and charter for a community that had not existed before. And each community lived in the conviction that God had spoken to it for the last time: the Jews, for the first and final time; the Christians, for the second and final time; the Muslims, for the third and final time.

The Bible, New Testament, and Qur'an, though looked upon as emanating from the same source, are very different works. The Bible is a rich and composite blend of religious myth, historical narrative, legal enactments, prophetic admonitions, cautionary tales, and poetry composed over a long span of time. The time span of the New Testament is considerably shorter, a half-century perhaps, but it too has a very mixed content of quasi [seeming to be] biography, community history, letters, and, in some versions, an apocalyptic Book of Revelation. The Qur'an, as we have seen, is absolutely contemporary to its revelation, twenty-two years in the lifetime of the Prophet.

There is nothing but God's own Word in the Qur'an, as Muhammad himself could assure the community of believers. In Jewish and Christian circles, however, there were assuredly circulating other writings that had some claim to being God's Word but are not found in the Bible or the New Testament. Both these Scriptures represent, then, a deliberate decision by someone to designate certain works as authentic or canonical Scripture and to exclude others from the canon. That decision was essentially theological, and the exclusion of the noncanonical writings, generally called Apocrypha, from the Jewish or Christian Scriptures does not render them any less interesting or important from a historical point of view. The Books of Maccabees never made it into the Jewish canon, for example, nor the Gnostic gospels into the Christian, but each tells us something of the events and attitudes of the time that produced them.

The Bible was originally composed in Hebrew, with some late passages in Aramaic, and is available in a variety of English translations, either alone or in combination with the New Testament. It is notable that where once sectarian differences among Jews, Catholics, and Protestants created marked discrepancies in their respective translations, the differences have presently narrowed to so few words or passages that it is possible for Jewish and Christian scholars to collaborate on such translation projects as the *Anchor Bible*.

There are in print a few English translations of the Qur'an, also commonly though somewhat less properly spelled Koran. The diction of the Qur'an is extremely elliptical [missing words from a sentence that would complete the construction] and any English version of it will, of course, sound far more alien to Western ears long attuned to the familiar rhythms and images of the Bible and the New Testament, but the most readable English translation, and one that catches some of the flavor of the original, is probably A.J. Arberry's *The Koran Interpreted*. Translation is also interpretation, as Arberry's title already suggests, and the virtue of *The Meaning of the Glorious Koran* by Mohammed Marmaduke Pickthall, an English convert to Islam, is that the translation reflects in fact a traditional Muslim interpretation of the text.

It is more than familiarity that makes both Bible and Gospels better served by their translations than is the Arabic Qu'ran. God's message to Muhammad was delivered in the highly charged, affective images of the sacred poet. It is allusive rather than explicit, a great body of warning, command, injunction, and instruction delivered against a background of men and manners as barren to our eyes as the steppe itself. We feel Sinai and Canaan in the Bible; Palestine, its houses, mountains, rivers and lakes, its towns and cities and the men who lived in them are all present in the Gospel narrative. In the Qur'an, however, we search without success for Mecca, for the profane but vividly commercial life of the Quraysh, for Muhammad's family and companions. In its pages there is only a voice, the voice of God alone. When it was heard, it overwhelmed hearts, as it still does in its written form, but it leaves the historian attending vainly, and deafly, for context.

The Concept of a Homeland

by Oscar I. Janowsky

The proclamation of the State of Israel in 1948 marked the confirmation of the bond that exists between the Jewish people and *Eretz Yisrael*, the land of Israel. This was the bond that had been begun during biblical times when the Israelites dwelled in the land of Canaan, a land they had occupied before their enslavement in Egypt and to which they returned under the leadership of Moses and Joshua. Jews look to the story of God's covenant with Abraham as told in the book of Genesis of the Bible as proof of their special relationship with the land of Israel: "I give the land you sojourn in to you and your offspring to come, all the land of Canaan, as an everlasting possession."

The following selection was written by the late Oscar I. Janowsky, formerly a professor of history at City College of the City University of New York. Janowsky describes how Zionism, the movement that called for a national homeland for the Jews, inspired and guided various agencies, organizations, and individuals to build a Jewish national home. That national home eventually became the State of Israel.

Oscar I. Janowsky, "The Rise of the State of Israel," *The Jews: Their Role in Civilization.* Edited by Louis Finkelstein. New York: Schocken Books, 1971. Copyright © 1971 by Louis Finkelstein. Reproduced by permission of Random House, Inc.

The Jews or Hebrews have been identified with Palestine—the Land of Israel—since patriarchal beginnings. For some 500 or 600 years, the entire Hebrew people dwelt in the Land of Israel. Between the eighth and sixth centuries B.C., the Diaspora [the exile of the Jews from Palestine after the Babylonian conquest of the Kingdom of Judah in 598 and 587 B.C.] developed, and increasing numbers of Jews lived outside the homeland. But Palestine remained the center of Jewish life during the Second Commonwealth [created by the Hasmoneans in the period from 167 B.C. to A.D. 63], and throughout that long period Jews in varying numbers continued to return to Palestine from the Diaspora. Even after the Romans sacked Jerusalem and burned the Second Temple in 70 C.E., the Jews of Palestine enjoyed a limited autonomy [self-rule] and continued to exert religious and cultural leadership over the Jews of foreign lands. After the fourth century C.E., persecution sapped the strength of Palestine Jewry and the population dwindled, but the idea persisted that the Jews and the Land of Israel were indissolubly linked to one another. Throughout the Middle Ages, and in modern times, too, small groups of Jews felt the need to "Return to Zion," and came to live in the Holy Land or at least to be buried in hallowed ground.

The lure of Palestine for the Jews endured through the long centuries of dispersion. The land was remembered as the cradle of early peoplehood. There the Jews had been welded into what we call today a nation. National triumphs and catastrophes, perpetuated in religious lore, remained associated with the country. Above all, the religious and literary genius of the Jews had blossomed in the Land of Israel, and it ever remained as the spiritual haven. In prayer and poetic yearning, in synagogue art and group imagery, the Land of Israel symbolized at once the glory of bygone days and the hope of redemption as a people.

The Zionist Movement

This set the stage for the Zionist movement of the late nineteenth and early twentieth centuries. The impulse came from within the Jewish group, primarily in Eastern Europe, where a cultural revival fostered national consciousness. The nationalist ferment among the submerged peoples of the area likewise affected the Jews, and the external pressures of anti-Semitism added a compulsive urge to return to Palestine and rebuild the old homeland. During the 1880's, groups of pioneers began to settle in Palestine, and an organized movement developed to encourage and sustain the settlers.

Theodor Herzl [1860–1904] gave dynamic leadership to the incipient Zionist movement. A Zionist Congress was held in Basle, Switzerland, in 1897, and a Zionist Organization was established with the aim of creating "for the Jewish people a home in Palestine secured by public law." An administrative apparatus was set up, an official journal founded, financial instruments established, and Herzl launched diplomatic and personal negotiations which brought Zionism to the attention of governments and public opinion. Herzl's activities were cut short by untimely death, but the Zionist movement endured. Jewish immigration to Palestine continued and by 1914 there were some 85,000 Jews in the country.

The First World War proved decisive in the history of Zionism. On November 2, 1917, the British government issued the Balfour Declaration, pledging to facilitate "the establishment in Palestine of a national home for

the Jewish People." Soon thereafter the British conquered the country and, when the war was over, Palestine was administered as a Mandate under the League of
Nations, with the United Kingdom as Mandatory or
trustee. The Balfour pledge was incorporated in the
terms of the Mandate, which recognized "the historical
connection of the Jewish people with Palestine" and the
right to reconstitute "their national home in that country." Britain was to encourage the immigration and
close settlement of Jews on the land; Hebrew (as well as
English and Arabic) was to be an official language; and
a "Jewish Agency" was to assist and co-operate with the
British in the building of the Jewish National Home.
The approval of the terms of the Mandate by the Council of the League of Nations gave international sanction
to the ideal of a Jewish National Home in Palestine.

These triumphs of Zionism appeared decisive, but
they proved insufficient for the realization of a viable
Jewish National Home. The fundamental need was
large-scale Jewish immigration, which depended on extensive economic development. The latter, however, required governmental powers which the Jews did not
possess.

The British wielded the powers of government, but
their primary objective was to advance imperial interests rather than Jewish national aspirations. Imperial interests required peace and stability in the Middle East
with tractable native populations and governments. If
the National Home could be built with Arab acquies-
cence, British good will would, no doubt, have been assured. But the Arabs opposed the National Home and
resorted to rioting and bloodshed. Since suppression
threatened to alienate the native population, the British
sought to placate the Arabs by restraining Jewish efforts.

The commitments of the Balfour Declaration and the Mandate included safeguards for the Arabs, and the British attempted to steer a course which they regarded as just to both peoples. However, as the Arab-Jewish conflict sharpened, that course veered away from the requirements of the Jewish National Home. The emphasis shifted, and the demands of the Arabs began to outweigh in British policy the positive injunctions to further the Jewish National Home.

Resistance to the Idea of a National Home

The Arabs proved the most formidable obstacle. Their leadership was imbued with the spirit of nationalism, and the masses were aroused to resist Jewish immigration and the entire idea of the National Home. The Jews argued that economic development increased the capacity of the country to absorb Jewish immigration without harm to the Arabs, and they adduced evidence that the latter profited from Jewish efforts. All to no effect. The Arab leadership repeatedly fomented violence, which taxed British patience, not so much with Arab resistance as with Jewish dynamism, which they came to regard as the cause of their difficulties.

In 1936, Arab riots broke out again and soon assumed the character of a national revolt. And in the late 1930's, world events predisposed the British to sacrifice the National Home to real or presumed imperial interests. The challenges of Hitler [leader of Nazi Germany] and Mussolini [leader of Fascist Italy] induced a policy of appeasement in Europe, in the Mediterranean, and in the Middle East. The Arabs, too, were to be appeased by the White Paper of 1939. The latter limited Jewish immigration to a total of 75,000 between

1939–1944, and thereafter the Jewish National Home was to be shut tight even against Jewish refugees, unless the Arabs approved. This was followed by drastic restrictions on land sales to Jews which barred further acquisition of land in 95 per cent of the area of Palestine. In the end, the Arabs were not appeased, but these measures committed the British to the scuttling of the Jewish National Home.

The Second World War taxed the statesmanship of Palestine Jewish leadership. They had no choice but to rally to the support of Britain, for the Nazis were the supreme enemy. However, the brutal enforcement of the White Paper of 1939 led to defiance. When the victims of Nazi terror perished for want of asylum, and when hapless refugees were turned away from the National Home, Palestine Jewry was bitterly resentful. Some elements resorted to terrorism, but among the Jewish population as a whole national discipline held. A threefold policy was evolved: co-operation in fighting the war was offered the British government; illegal immigration was encouraged in defiance of the British authorities; and the desire for a National Home hardened into a demand for statehood.

A National Home Evolves

The Jews were obliged to expend much effort in defending their policies, in presenting evidence before the numerous British commissions of inquiry, and in pleading their cause in Palestine, England, and elsewhere. But their best energies were devoted to constructive work and, despite all hindrances, remarkable progress was made in the building of the Jewish National Home.

The work of building was guided by various agencies, some of which had the support of non-Zionists. But the most important were the instruments of the world Zionist movement. The leading body was the Zionist Organization, or the Jewish Agency (after 1929), which had the right under the Mandate of advising and co-operating with the British authorities on matters affecting the National Home. It mobilized the support of Jews and others, negotiated with the British, and represented the cause of the National Home before the organs of the League of Nations [a peace-keeping organization founded after World War I]. The Palestine Executive of this body set up administrative departments which dealt with immigration, agricultural settlement, trade and industry, labor, education, health, and other functions.

The *Keren Hayesod* and the Jewish National Fund were the chief financial instruments. The former raised over £P18,000,000 between 1920–1946 (59 per cent in the United States), and figured in the financing of almost every important effort relating to the building of the National Home. The Jewish National Fund purchased land as the "possession of the Jewish people"; in 1945–1946, it held over 213,000 acres—about 44 per cent of all land owned by Jews.

Numerous other agencies co-operated in the development of the National Home. Baron Edmond de Rothschild of Paris had generously supported the early agricultural settlements, and in the 1920's the Palestine Jewish Colonization Association (PICA) took over his holdings and continued his work. By 1945, the Rothschild and PICA activities had resulted in the acquisition of about 123,000 acres and the founding or support of some forty settlements.

Hadassah, the Women's Zionist Organization of America, concentrated its efforts on public health and medical service, in which it became a major influence in the country. It maintained hospitals and clinics; pioneered in child welfare, nurses' training, preventive medicine, and the care of the tubercular; and cooperated in antimalaria and other health efforts. The Women's International Zionist Organization (WIZO) engaged mainly in the training of pioneer women in agricultural, vocational, and homemaking functions.

Business organizations worked with private capital independently of the Zionist bodies. One example was the Palestine Economic Corporation, which participated in financing large undertakings, such as the Palestine Potash Company and the Palestine Electric Corporation. Finally, Palestine Jewry developed numerous agencies, notably the *Histadrut* or General Federation of Labor, which shared in the work of building, and profoundly affected the character of the Jewish National Home. . . .

Economic expansion was not uncommon in underdeveloped countries after the First World War. What made Palestine unique was the national and social setting in which the economy functioned. The National Home was not built on cheap labor, its architects were not dominated by the urge for profits, and the financial backers were motivated by national idealism or philanthropy rather than by gain. There was experimentation with co-operative institutions and a widespread conviction that social stability and change must rest on respect for human personality, individual freedom, and democratic processes.

The dominating ideal was national rebirth, and *halutziut*, or dedicated pioneering, the means of its realiza-

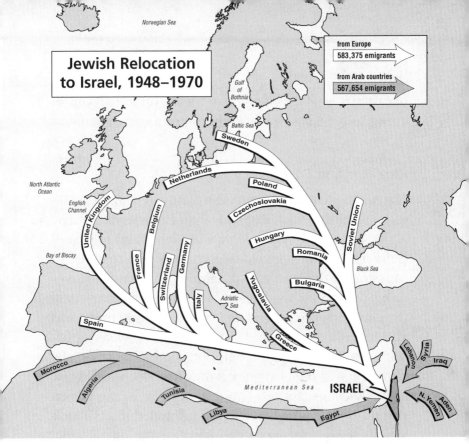

Jewish Relocation to Israel, 1948–1970

from Europe
583,375 emigrants

from Arab countries
567,654 emigrants

tion. The Hebrew language was revived, so that in 1948 over 75 per cent of Palestine Jewry above two years of age spoke Hebrew, and over 93 per cent of all children aged two to fourteen employed it as their vernacular [everyday language]. The traditional Jewish faith in education was reflected in a far-flung voluntary system which imparted some elementary education to about 90 per cent of the Jewish children, and which expended in 1944–1945 nearly four times the Palestine government's education budget. The Hebrew University and the Haifa Institute of Technology were founded when the National Home was little more than a hope and a half-promise. Adult education in the form of evening courses, lectures, and tours brought knowledge to the isolated settlements as well as the urban centers. And Hebrew culture, the press, the theater, music, and the plastic arts were developed to a high level in two generations by a heterogeneous immigrant population. . . .

Idealism and Democracy

The unique feature of the Jewish National Home was the social idealism which inspired large segments of the Jewish population. Physical labor—self-labor and toil especially on the land—was idealized as the preferred means of restoring the land and reclaiming the people. Novel forms of group living were evolved in the collective settlements (the *kvutzot* and *kibbutzim*), in which property and income, production and distribution, were socialized. And this was done without compulsion, because human needs rather than preconceived doctrines determined social evolution. Those who preferred less pervasive forms of co-operative living fashioned the Workers Smallholders' Settlement (*Moshav Ovdim*) and the Collective Smallholders' Settlement (*Moshav Shitufi*), which combined individualized family living with varying degrees of collective production, or joined middle-class settlements, where co-operation was limited to joint purchasing, marketing, water supply, and the like. . . .

Democracy, too, was a distinctive feature of the Jewish National Home. The atmosphere of Jewish Palestine was democratic. Equality was a working principle of social relationships; respect for human personality and for individual differences prevailed; above all, freedom to differ and to express varying points of view was maintained. And voluntarism rather than compulsion governed political, social, and economic life. Jewish Palestine was not a utopia, but diverse elements were able to work together in relative peace in the building of the Jewish National Home.

CHAPTER 2

Basic Beliefs of Judaism

The Oneness of God

by Milton Steinberg

In Judaism, God has many attributes. Among these, he is the playwright, leading character, and director of the human drama. Above all, he is one. So says Milton Steinberg, scholar, rabbi, and author of the following selection. God is *the* cornerstone of Judaism, a faith that established the supremacy, realness, and all-enveloping "oneness" of the deity. As pointed out by Steinberg, this singularity was in profound opposition to other religions of the ancient world. They were constructed around the worship of many diverse deities (polytheism), or a deity with dual natures (as in the case of Zoroastrianism), or a singular deity manifested in three entities (as in the case of Christianity). Scholars try to assign a name to the God-centeredness of Judaism. Milton Steinberg uses the term "God-faith." The oneness of God is the theme of this excerpt taken from Steinberg's book *Basic Judaism*.

Steinberg was born in 1903 in Rochester, New York, and died in 1950 at the age of forty-six. Steinberg began his career as a rabbi of a Conservative synagogue in Indianapolis. In 1933 he moved to the Park Avenue Synagogue in New York City. There he began to depart from Conservative Judaism in favor of Reconstructionism, then a school of Judaism but now a fourth denomination after Orthodox, Conservative, and Reform Judaism. Steinberg believed that Reconstructionism, with its belief in the evolutionary nature of Jewish civilization, combined the best of Jewish tradition with the intellectual advances of the twentieth century. A brilliant sermonizer, Steinberg was also a persuasive writer. His most famous work is *Basic Judaism*, first published in 1947. This volume was written for Jews and non-Jews alike. His other works include *The Making of the Modern Jew*, *A Believing Jew: The Selected Writings of Milton Steinberg*, and the historical novel, *As a Driven Leaf.*

One assertion the Jewish religion makes concerning God, which, by the testimony of the Tradition itself, is the very cornerstone of Jewish theology:

It says of God that He is one.

This seemingly simple statement cuts deeper and runs richer than first appears. Its meanings are many and important. Of these, furthermore, each successive epoch [a time of major change] called one or another into prominence, thus investing the single self-same affirmation with different primary significances for different generations. Yet each of these is no more than an aspect of the rounded and continuing Jewish God-faith; taken in succession they epitomize Jewish theology. On both scores they are worth reviewing.

These are the significances which history from time to time has extracted from God's oneness.

God is one, and not many.

The ancient world was polytheistic [believing in many gods] both as to nature and as to society.

Heathendom assumed a deity in and for each object: the river, the tree, the sun; in and for each faculty and function: fertility, memory, the artisan's skill. So it tore reality to shreds, and then, to confound confusion, assumed that each spirit had no other role except to look after its own. Under this construction there was no order, either logical or moral, to things.

In the same fashion paganism, [neither Jew, Muslim nor Christian] positing a separate deity for each people, territory, and economic class, tore mankind also to shreds. For, just as a subject and his king owed political loyalty to each another and no one else, so with the relationship between a national god and his worshipers: each was expected to look out for his own exclusively, without regard for anyone else. Thus ancient religion rationalized the lawlessness of ancient society, legitimatizing the exploitation of all who stood outside the pale [boundary] of protection of the local deity and lending supernatural sanctions to any attempt by the god-favored nation against its neighbors.

In proclaiming the oneness of God, therefore, the prophets intended more than a repudiation of idol worship. They were bent on establishing the principles that reality is an order, not an anarchy; that mankind is a unity, not a hodge-podge; and that one universal law of righteousness holds sway over men, transcending borders, surmounting all class lines.

At the same time and with even greater practical import their monotheism constituted a declaration of war against spiritual idolatry in all its forms: the worship to which man is addicted of the self and its desires, or of caste and group interest, or of the state and the autarch [absolute ruler] in whom it may take on symbolic embodiment. Having proclaimed the Lord alone to be God, they asserted in effect that to Him only and to His law of righteousness supremacy is to be ascribed and unreserved loyalty to be accorded.

God is one, not two.

Sometime in the sixth century before the Common Era [before the birth of Christ], Judaism met Zoroastrianism [a religion founded by Zoroaster, a Persian], encountering for the first time a religion rivaling itself in maturity, spirituality, and earnestness. Distinctive of this faith was its doctrine of dualism. Behind the world it discerned not one but two creative beings, the first a force of light and goodness, the other a power of darkness and evil. These twin genii [supernatural spirits] wrestle ceaselessly for the world and man's soul, a struggle in which each human being, willy-nilly, takes sides. Religion's purpose, as Zoroastrianism conceived it, is to make certain that men choose the right side.

This theology has its attractions. It is dramatic in its picture of a world conflict, heroic in the demands it makes of man, and metaphysically alluring, since it offers—or seems to offer—a quick solution to the enigma of evil.

Despite all this, Judaism rejected it. Whatever its advantages, the disabilities of dualism proved greater.

Dualism makes an absolute of evil; Judaism regards evil as contingent to a prior and more basic good.

Dualism despairs in advance of half of reality and half of human nature. Judaism holds that there is nothing which cannot be retrieved for the good. The most sinful impulses in man, as the rabbis point out, are the very forces which, properly directed, motivate the virtues.

Dualism places the ultimate triumph of the good in jeopardy. If the dark be correlative to the light, what assurance is there that the latter will prevail?

Judaism's repudiation of Zoroastrianism was not achieved in a moment. For centuries the possibility of "two powers" continued to tempt the Jewish imagination. But the first reaction of the prophet when he insisted that one and the same God "fashions light and creates darkness, makes peace and creates evil,"—that remained in the end the Tradition's last word.

God is one, not three.

During the Middle Ages the Jewish assertion of God's unity became an explicit denial of the Christian dogma of the Trinity, a total disavowal of the thesis that God, though one, is somehow at the same time three persons, "coeternal and coequal."

In rejecting this doctrine Jews were concerned primarily with warding off what they regarded as a misrepresentation of the Divine nature. But they were no less zealous to indicate their dissent from the notion, integral to the Trinity, of a God-man: Deity embodied in the flesh and blood of some particular individual. To them all men reflect God's nature and are His children. The suggestion that any single human being might be God Himself they spurned as blasphemy [extreme irreverence].

God is one, not none.

So in our day Judaism declares its unyielding opposition to contemporary atheism and the materialism that attends it; to the new, yet old, misreading of reality as the blind interplay of matter and energy; to the error that man and his values are children of cosmic chance, destined to perish as pointlessly as they came to be.

So also the Tradition protests against another and scarcely less dangerous modern fallacy, the evasive proposition that God *is* but does not *exist*, that He is only a human conception or a useful fiction, or that His name may properly be assigned to the highest value a man cherishes. Against all such slippery counsels Judaism affirms that God's existence is independent of man and that He is not only actual and real but the most actual actuality and realest reality of all.

In the end then, the Tradition at the latest stage in its career takes its stand again on the same verity which first gave it life and character.

Judaism says further concerning God:

—That He is the *Creator* of all things through all time, Nor is His creativity to be viewed as a lone episode in the past, a tossing out, as it were, of the cosmic ball which is then allowed to roll where it will. On the contrary, He continues to sustain and animate the universe, ever evoking new things and regenerating the old, even as the prayerbook asserts: "He reneweth in His goodness, every day continually, the work of Creation."

—That He is *Spirit*, which is to say, that He is at one and the same time a Mind that contemplates and a Power at work. To put it in different words, that He is Reason and Purpose.

It is in this respect that man, instinct with thought and will, is closest akin to God. Wherefore the medieval philosopher-poet, Solomon ibn Gabirol, [1021–1058] enumerating the "three things which stand together to bring the awareness of Thee ever before me," lists first the heavens and second the earth in its expanse, but as a climactic third "the stirring of my heart when I look inward."

—That He is *Lawgiver*, and that in three senses.

He is the source not only of the natural law to which the physical world conforms but also of the moral law regulative of human existence.

He is the mind disclosed in revelation.

He is the guarantor of morality, the rectifier of disturbed balances, and the power that enforces the right.

—That He is the *Guide of History.*

To Judaism history is the unfolding of a design of

which the dénouement [final outcome] is to be man's ultimate fulfillment and redemption.

Behind this drama stands God: playwright, director, animator, spectator, critic, and—from within every character and setting—actor also. Wherefore the Tradition speaks frequently of Him as the God of the Patriarchs, of the Exodus, and of Sinai; that is, of the past; or in terms of His Kingdom to come, of the future; in sum, as the God of the cosmic and the human adventure.

—That He is man's *Helper.*

God's assistance to man is not to be espied only or even primarily in spectacular and crucial incidents. It is much more a matter of what the traditional prayerbook describes as "Thy miracles which are daily with us, Thy wonders and goodnesses which are wrought at all time, evening, morn, and noon"; that is to say, of the normalities of human experience.

Thus God is forever helping man through the resources and dependability of the physical world.

He helps man further through man's own body, skilled, adaptable, resilient; through his mind, eager and ingenious; through his heart, life-loving, courageous, and aspiring.

He helps man through the medium of other men; their capacity for cooperation; the social wealth and technical informations they have amassed together; the love and understanding they afford one another; the political devices and civil liberties which protect them in life and freedom; . . .

—That He is the *Liberator* of men and their societies.

God is the Power working within individuals and people that will not permit them to acquiesce in servitude, their own or that of others. He is the spark that kindles them into rebellion and the iron that makes them stubborn for freedom's sake. And simultaneously He hardens the heart of tyrants, until lost to reason, incapable of either learning or forgetting, they destroy themselves.

Of God's emancipations [freeing] all peoples have had experience but Israel especially, most particularly when it was brought forth from Egypt by a mighty hand and an outstretched arm. Wherefore the Exodus [the freeing of the Israelites from slavery in Egypt] is to Jews, as indeed to much of mankind, the classic instance of liberation; a proof that since God *is*, every bondage [enslavement] political, economic, or spiritual, can be and someday will be broken.

—That He is the *Savior* of souls.

Men may be enslaved not only from without but by inner blindness, weakness, and perversity. External deliverance therefore does not suffice; there is need of salvation also.

Salvation, as the Tradition construes [understands] it, may pertain to life-after-death; its primary reference, however, from the Jewish viewpoint, is to this world.

Salvation is man's victory over his limitations: ignorance, for instance, or insensitivity; it is his conquest of sinfulness, of the evils resident within him, such as pride, selfishness, hate, lust, cynicism, the deliberate rejection of goodness and truth.

Against these and other perversions, God stands as Savior. The very awareness of Him is a saving power, helping to emancipate the human spirit from the restraints that frustrate it, from the wickednesses that corrupt it from within. All the more, He Himself, now driving man relentlessly by *force majeure*, now leading him gently—even guilefully—but ever and constantly moving him to the redemption of his soul.

The Covenant Between God and the Hebrews

from the Book of Exodus

A covenant is an agreement or binding contract between two parties. In the ancient Middle East, covenants were used as legal documents and were usually sealed by some kind of ceremonial act such as an oath or a meal. The concept of covenant has great importance in Judaism and is central to its beliefs and development. Jews believe that for the first time in human history, God forged a personal bond between himself and a people. This bond bypasses the rules of a king or the interventions of a priestly caste. There are great responsibilities for the people who share in the covenant, however. As recipients of God's laws, or commandments, they are responsible for the observance of the law.

The Hebrew Bible or Tanakh tells of several covenants between God and his creation. As told in the book of Genesis, for example, God grants to Abraham and his descendants the land of Canaan to hold for all time. The book of Exodus recounts how Moses and the Israelites arrive at Mount Sinai after their escape from slavery in Egypt. Moses climbs the mountain and receives from God a decree to set up a covenant by which the Israelites will obey God and in return be considered unique among the peoples of the world. The Israelites

Tanakh: A New Translation of the Holy Scriptures According to the Traditional Hebrew Text. Philadelphia: The Jewish Publication Society, 1985. Copyright © 1985 by The Jewish Publication Society. All rights reserved. Reproduced by permission.

agree and receive, through Moses, a list of God's commandments or laws to follow. The story of the covenant established on Mount Sinai is viewed by Jewish theologians as a fundamental doctrine of the faith.

The selection from the book of Exodus that follows describes Moses' return to Mount Sinai after he smashed the first set of tablets containing the commandments given by God to the Israelites. Moses was angered by the people's worship of a golden calf during his absence. In the following passages, God restates his covenant with the Israelites and expands upon his commandments.

The LORD said to Moses: "Carve two tablets of stone like the first, and I will inscribe upon the tablets the words that were on the first tablets, which you shattered. Be ready by morning, and in the morning come up to Mount Sinai and present yourself there to Me, on the top of the mountain. No one else shall come up with you, and no one else shall be seen anywhere on the mountain; neither shall the flocks and the herds graze at the foot of this mountain."

So Moses carved two tablets of stone, like the first, and early in the morning he went up on Mount Sinai, as the LORD had commanded him, taking the two stone tablets with him. The LORD came down in a cloud; He stood with him there, and proclaimed the name LORD. The LORD passed before him and proclaimed: "The LORD! the LORD! a God compassionate and gracious, slow to anger, abounding in kindness and faithfulness, extending kindness to the thousandth generation, forgiving iniquity [wickedness], transgression, and sin; yet He does not remit [cancel] all punishment, but visits the iniquity of parents upon children and children's children, upon the third and fourth generation."

Moses hastened to bow low to the ground in homage, and said, "If I have gained Your favor, O Lord, pray, let the Lord go in our midst, even though this is a stiff-necked people. Pardon our iniquity and our sin, and take us for Your own!"

"I Hereby Make a Covenant"

He said: I hereby make a covenant. Before all your people I will work such wonders as have not been wrought on all the earth or in any nation; and all the people who are with you shall see how awesome are the LORD's deeds which I will perform for you. Mark well what I command you this day. I will drive out before you the Amorites, the Canaanites, the Hittites, the Perizzites, the Hivites, and the Jebusites [all peoples of the ancient Middle East]. Beware of making a covenant with the inhabitants of the land against which you are advancing, lest they be a snare [trap] in your midst. No, you must tear down their altars, smash their pillars, and cut down their sacred posts; for you must not worship any other god, because the LORD, whose name is Impassioned, is an impassioned God. You must not make a covenant with the inhabitants of the land, for they will lust after their gods and sacrifice to their gods and invite you; and you will eat of their sacrifices. And when you take wives from among their daughters for your sons, their daughters will lust after their gods and will cause your sons to lust after their gods.

You shall not make molten [metal] gods for yourselves.

You shall observe the Feast of Unleavened Bread

[Passover]—eating unleavened bread for seven days, as I have commanded you—at the set time of the month of Abib, for in the month of Abib you went forth from Egypt.

Every first issue of the womb is Mine, from all your livestock that drop a male as firstling, whether cattle or sheep. But the firstling of an ass you shall redeem with a sheep; if you do not redeem it, you must break its neck. And you must redeem every first-born among your sons.

None shall appear before Me empty-handed.

Six days you shall work, but on the seventh day you shall cease from labor; you shall cease from labor even at plowing time and harvest time.

You shall observe the Feast of Weeks, of the first fruits of the wheat harvest; and the Feast of Ingathering at the turn of the year. Three times a year all your males shall appear before the Sovereign LORD, the God of Israel. I will drive out nations from your path and enlarge your territory; no one will covet [desire] your land when you go up to appear before the LORD your God three times a year.

You shall not offer the blood of My sacrifice with anything leavened; and the sacrifice of the Feast of Passover shall not be left lying until morning.

The choice first fruits of your soil you shall bring to the house of the LORD your God.

You shall not boil a kid [baby goat] in its mother's milk.

And the LORD said to Moses: Write down these commandments, for in accordance with these commandments I make a covenant with you and with Israel.

And he was there with the LORD forty days and forty nights; he ate no bread and drank no water; and he wrote down on the tablets the terms of the covenant, the Ten Commandments.

Moses Returns to the People

So Moses came down from Mount Sinai. And as Moses came down from the mountain bearing the two tablets of the Pact, Moses was not aware that the skin of his face was radiant, since he had spoken with Him! Aaron [Moses' brother] and all the Israelites saw that the skin of Moses' face was radiant; and they shrank from coming near him. But Moses called to them, and Aaron and all the chieftains in the assembly returned to him, and Moses spoke to them. Afterward all the Israelites came near, and he instructed them concerning all that the LORD had imparted to him on Mount Sinai. And when Moses had finished speaking with them, he put a veil over his face.

Whenever Moses went in before the LORD to speak with Him, he would leave the veil off until he came out; and when he came out and told the Israelites what he had been commanded, the Israelites would see how radiant the skin of Moses' face was. Moses would then put the veil back over his face until he went in to speak with Him.

Love Thy Neighbor as Thyself

by Jacob Neusner

Judaism demands that its adherents study the Torah, the Laws as contained in the Bible, and fulfill the commandments described therein. These are the commandments that God revealed to Moses on Mount Sinai as the expression of his covenant with the Israelites. Fulfillment of the commandments means, among many other things, obeying the will of God, imitating God, and living a life that glorifies him. Such a life is a good life.

The guidelines for living a good life are addressed by God to the Israelites in the Torah but are intended for all humanity. They are made explicit in the biblical imperative to "love thy neighbor as thyself." In the following selection Jacob Neusner describes Judaism's ethical imperative of selflessness, using examples from stories told by famous rabbis, Jewish religious authorities and teachers.

Neusner is research professor of religion and theology at Bard College, Annandale-on-Hudson, New York. He has lectured and written extensively on Judaism. His written works include *Torah Through the Ages: A Short History of Judaism* and *Recovering Judaism: The Universal Dimension of Jewish Religion.*

The main point of the Torah, stated simply, is this: the Torah, written and oral, aims at transforming Adam into Israel, and Israel into God's image, after God's likeness, which was God's original plan. But God created all humanity 'in our image, after our likeness', and the qualities that in humanity replicate God's traits cannot, therefore, be set forth in language particular to Israel. Ethical imperatives are addressed by God in the Torah to Israel, but they pertain to all humanity, defining what it means to be a human being. The Talmud [the entire body of Jewish tradition] phrases what is at stake in simple sayings such as, 'The All-Merciful wants the heart', 'The commandments were given only to purify humanity', and the like. Scripture itself is explicit: 'You shall not hate your brother in your heart, but you shall reason with your neighbour, lest you bear sin because of him. You shall not take vengeance or bear any grudge against the sons of your own people, but you shall love your neighbour as yourself: I am the Lord' (Leviticus 19:17–18), which some authorities, in particular Hillel [ca. 70 B.C.–A.D. 10] the great Pharisaic master of the turn of the first century, identify as the most important law of the Torah.

> ' . . . but you shall love your neighbor as yourself: I am the Lord':
>
> Rabbi Akiva says, 'This is the encompassing principle of the Torah.'
>
> Rabbi ben Azzai says, '"This is the book of the generations of Adam" (Genesis 5:1) is a still more encompassing principle [because that verse proves all humanity shares a common ancestry and forms a single family].'

Right takes priority over rite, as the prophets make

clear, and saving a life trumps [overrides] all other religious obligations and commandments. These sayings, with their insistence on right attitude, one in which the heart of the human being willingly accedes to the will of God, stand no great distance from the story of Adam and Eve in Eden and Israel at Sinai, rebelling against God while Moses was yet on the mountain.

What Matters Most

As far as the weight of Judaic teaching, from Scripture onwards, is concerned, what matters most is ethical conduct towards one's fellow human being. That is at the heart of Judaism's story of the good life. A famous story leaves no question that right action towards other people is how the entire Torah is best summed up:

> There was the case of a gentile [non-Jew] who came before Shammai [the colleague and opponent of Hillel]. He said to him, 'Convert me on the stipulation that you teach me the entire Torah while I am standing on one foot.' He drove him off with the measuring rod that he had in his hand.
>
> He came before Hillel: 'Convert me.'
>
> He said to him, '"What is hateful to you, don't do to your fellow." That's the entire Torah; all the rest is commentary, Now go, study.'

Hillel is paraphrasing Leviticus 19:17–18; since the rest of the Torah elaborates that point, one should go and study the Torah to learn what is required in order to keep this golden rule.

More often than not, the highest virtue is goodwill, which encompasses every other social virtue of generosity, foresight, neighbourliness, and the rest. The worst vice is not envy, bad neighbourliness or defaulting on a loan, but ill-will, which generates all other vices:

> [Rabbi Yohanan ben Zakai, the rabbinic sage] said to them, 'Go and see what is the straight path to which someone should stick.'
>
> Rabbi Eliezer says, 'A generous spirit.'
>
> Rabbi Joshua says, 'A good friend.'
>
> Rabbi Yose says, 'A good neighbour,'
>
> Rabbi Simeon says, 'Foresight.'
>
> Rabbi Eleazar says, 'Goodwill.'
>
> He said to them, 'I prefer the opinion of Rabbi Eleazar ben Arakh, because in what he says is included everything you say.'
>
> He said to them, 'Go out and see what is the bad road, which someone should avoid.'
>
> Rabbi Eliezer says, 'Envy.'
>
> Rabbi Joshua says, 'A bad friend.'
>
> Rabbi Yose says, 'A bad neighbour.'
>
> Rabbi Simeon says, 'Defaulting on a loan.'
>
> (A loan owed to a human being and a loan owed to the Omnipresent, blessed be he, are the same, as it is said, 'The wicked person borrows and cannot pay back, but the righteous person is generous and gives' [Psalm 37:21].)
>
> Rabbi Eleazar says, 'Ill will.'
>
> He said to them, 'I prefer the opinion of Rabbi Eleazar ben Arakh, because in what he says is included everything you say.'

The sage Rabbi Yohanan ben Zakai sees goodwill as the source of all specific virtues because in his view attitude and intention in the end define the human being: we are what we want to be; the world is what we want to make of it. The entire message of the Torah for the virtuous man and woman is summed up in that conviction, which, furthermore, is embodied in the law of Judaism governing the social order.

Acting in a Selfless Way

But what God really admires is acts of selflessness. That is because these form the opposite of arrogance. The highest virtue of all, so far as the Torah is concerned, is the act that God cannot coerce but very much yearns for, which is the act of love that transcends the self. That is the point of the Shema [basic statement of the Jewish faith] when it says, 'You shall love the Lord your God with all your heart, and with all your soul, and with all your might', the commandment of love. But love cannot be commanded, it can only be given freely. That is why virtue begins in sincere obedience to the Torah, but reaches its pinnacle through deeds beyond the strict requirements of obedience, and even the limits of the law altogether.

A set of sublime stories convey that principle. To understand the basis for the rabbinic sages' view, we have to keep in mind two facts. First, they believed that God hears and answers prayer, and that if God answers prayer, it is a mark of his favourable recognition of the one who says it. Therefore if someone has the reputation of saying prayers that are answered, the sages want to know why. Second, they believed that Torah-study defined the highest ideal that a man could attain, and they maintained that God wanted them to live a life of Torah-study. But in these stories, they discover people who could pray with effect in ways that the sages themselves could not. And they further discovered that some people win God's favour not by lifelong devotion to divine service but by doing a single remarkable action. So the sages themselves tell us stories about how one enormous deed can outweigh a life of Torah-study. The first story concerns a poor man who asked for charity:

> A certain man came before one of the relatives of Rabbi Yannai. He said to him. 'Rabbi, attain *zekut* through me [by giving me charity].'
>
> He said to him, 'And didn't your father leave you money?'
>
> He said to him, 'No.'
>
> He said to him, 'Go and collect what your father left on deposit with others.'
>
> He said to him, 'I have heard concerning property my father deposited with others that it was gained by violence [so I don't want it].'
>
> He said to him, 'You are worthy of praying and having your prayers answered.'

The word *zekut* means 'merit' or 'source of divine favour'. It is the language that is used by the beggar to the donor: you will gain merit by an act of philanthropy to me. This is self-evidently a reference to the possession of entitlement to God's favour, and it is gained, we see, through deeds that the law of the Torah cannot require but must favour: what one does of one's own volition [will] beyond the measure of the law. Here we see the opposite of sin. A sin is what one has done of one's own volition beyond all limits of the law. So an act that generates *zekut* for the individual is the counterpart and opposite: what one does of one's own volition that also is beyond all requirements of the law. . . .

An act of pure selflessness . . . is what gains for a man God's deepest interest. The ultimate act of virtue turns out to be an act of pure grace, to which God responds with pure grace. The extraordinary person is the one who sacrifices for the other in an act of selfless love, and that can be anybody, at any time, anywhere. That is why, for Judaism, the great commandment is one of love: 'You shall love the Lord your God with all your heart, and with all your soul, and with all your might,' as the creed of Judaism maintains. The one thing one person cannot command of another person is love. That, by definition, is freely given, or not given at all. Then virtue consists in doing on one's own what God yearns for but cannot impose, which is, to love God. That defines the goal of the Torah, and whether attained in a lifetime of study or in a single instance makes no difference.

The Role of Prayer

by David S. Ariel

In Judaism prayer is the act of expressing one's relationship with God. Prayer can be words recited by a group gathered together in the synagogue, Judaism's place of worship, or spoken by the individual at home. There are specific prayers for daily recitation during the week; on the Sabbath, the day of rest; and on holy days. In the Orthodox, or traditional, branch of Judaism prayer is carried out in the morning, afternoon, and in the evening. Ideally, prayers are recited by a minyan, a quorum of ten adult males. The Bible contains perhaps the most famous prayers ever composed, the book of Psalms. The psalms—hymns of praise, expressions of sorrow, or reflections on specific topics—comprise part of the liturgy of public worship services in the synagogue.

No matter where or when they pray, Jews believe that God hears and responds to prayer. In the following selection, David S. Ariel explains the meaning and importance of prayer in Judaism. The recitation of prayers in the group setting of the synagogue reaffirms Jews' sense of community and communicates Jewish values across generations, according to Ariel. Regular prayer, carried out over a period of time, also helps shape beliefs. Most important is the conviction with which a prayer is performed. A prayer recited without attentiveness and belief is meaningless.

David S. Ariel, *What Do Jews Believe? The Spiritual Foundations of Judaism*. New York: Schocken Books, 1995. Copyright © 1995 by David S. Ariel. All rights reserved. Reproduced by permission of Random House, Inc.

Ariel is president of the Cleveland College of Jewish Studies in Beechwood, Ohio. His works include *The Mystic Quest: An Introduction to Jewish Mysticism.*

Prayer is predicated on the sacred myth that God hears us and cares about us. Prayer is the service of our heart, expressing our deepest aspirations and the hope that we will be heard.

Prayer is a universal and deeply personal impulse which is expressed in many spontaneous ways. In Judaism, prayer is also a *mitzvah* [religious duty] that requires that a Jew pray three times daily according to a fixed liturgy from the Siddur, the Hebrew prayer book, and offer specific blessings at various moments throughout the day. Jews often express their most deeply personal feelings in silent prayer, while public prayers meet the halakhic [legally binding] requirements of Judaism. Judaism strikes a balance between personal spontaneity and public formality in prayer.

Jewish prayer expresses and articulates the sacred myths of Judaism in words that can be understood by all. The reinforcement of what Jews should believe occurs through the regular repetition of the words of the prayers in their original Hebrew or in English translation. If the performance of the *mitzvot* [plural of *mitzvah*] is the spiritual means of achieving transcendence through our behavior, prayer is the means of expressing out spiritual beliefs about transcendence through words.

Jews believe that prayer is one of the *mitzvot* but also that it transcends the other *mitzvot*. Prayer in Judaism is seen as more than an expression of belief. It provides a sense of belonging to a community and affirms one's

Jewishness in a social context. Being together in a synagogue with others who share our beliefs is often more
important than the meaning of the words themselves.
The synagogue is more than a house of prayer—it is the
place where we affirm out values within a social context. Each congregation represents a slightly different
social context, and so we tend to affiliate with the congregation that best reflects our values. Synagogues also
communicate Jewish values across generations. Congregations provide a valuable social message because
the synagogue is the only institution in Jewish life
where entire families are brought together with other
families. Although many secular contexts for expressing one's Jewishness are available through social-
welfare and voluntary associations, the nature of the
religious community is unique.

Religious rituals such as prayer not only express but
actually shape our beliefs. Traditional Jewish prayer involves a surrender to a mode of consciousness quite different from routine consciousness. To the involved
worshiper, attention to the service itself necessitates a
receptivity to stimuli not encountered anywhere else.
The physical sensation of singing, the presence of unusual ritual objects, the use of the Hebrew language,
the codes, signals, and rituals of the service, and the in-
vocation of religious concepts all contribute to the
transformation of routine consciousness. If this in-
volvement is sustained over time, it can produce a
sense of connectedness to the other worshipers and
spiritual fulfillment. Eventually, participation in regular prayer can shape our beliefs through repetition, routine, and reinforcement of the spiritual message.

Jews traditionally believe that prayer is meaningful
not only because it expresses what we believe but also

because it works. Some believe that prayer works because God listens, while others think that it primarily has a profound effect on us. Many people pray spontaneously at different moments in their lives or when they experience inner feelings on a deep level. This has been called variously praying, wishing, pouring out one's heart, conducting an interior conversation, or meditation. Spontaneous prayer is one of the deepest and most personal forms of human expression because it takes place privately and often unconsciously. It has always been an important part of Jewish spirituality.

The proper Hebrew term for what is called, incorrectly, "prayer" in English is *tefillah*. The word is derived from the Hebrew root *pll*, which means "to judge," "to intercede on behalf of someone," or "to hope." *Tefillah* there-

Jews gather to pray at the Wailing Wall in Jerusalem, the most sacred place in the Jewish religion.

fore implies an act of self-judgment or intercession on one's own behalf before God, or the expression of hopeful sentiments. *Tefillah* is the standard Jewish term referring both to the liturgical dimension of Judaism and to the spontaneous outpouring of the human heart. There is no good English equivalent for the word. The act of praying is also called *davening* in Yiddish [language consisting of Hebrew and German words and spoken by European Jews from the medieval period up to the World War II period].

Three Types of Prayers

Jewish liturgy is largely based on three types of prayers: thanksgiving (*hodayah*), praise (*tehillah*), and request (*bakashah*). Although each genre has a different purpose, the content of many of the prayers is similar, and they express a consistent system of Jewish beliefs. Many of the prayers reflect the rabbinic understanding of Judaism. What Jews believe today is often different from what the rabbis of earlier times believed. Since Jewish belief is continually evolving and not static, there is considerable room for doubt about, disagreement with, and even reformulation of rabbinic beliefs expressed in traditional Jewish prayers found in the Siddur. Before we look at how more recent Jewish beliefs are expressed in prayer, we will begin with how the sacred myths of rabbinic Judaism make praying possible and are expressed in the words we utter.

Traditional Jewish prayer expresses the belief that God existed alone before He created the world and will exist long after the world might cease to exist. God is the creator, sustainer, and ruler of the world. He established the rhythms of nature and set the regular patterns of night and day, the four seasons, birth and death. At any moment, God could withdraw His support from the world and allow it to collapse. Because of His love for the world, He constantly regenerates and renews life. In comparison to God, all human artifice and invention are inferior; all human rulers and earthly kings are flawed and insignificant. No other being is worthy of our recognition or praise. In our very existence we are the proof of God's perfection. We have been created with a pure soul and body, making us the pinnacle of creation. We testify to God's majesty in what we say and do. We are created in the image of God—but He is the potter and we are the clay.

The rabbis believed that even though we were created in the image of God, we often lose our way. Jewish prayer reiterates the belief that God will nevertheless have mercy on us and forgive our sins because He is a compassionate being who remembers His covenant [agreement and bond] with our ancestors. We frequently recall the covenant, the gift of Torah [the Law] and the historical events that remind us of God's love. In prayer, we recommit ourselves to do God's will and live a life of righteousness and goodness. Although our moral fate is in our hands, we turn to God and ask Him to protect us from illness, oppression, and catastrophe. We may not understand why we suffer, but we still have confidence in God's goodness. We ask for strength as we work to overcome our human faults, for forgiveness for our failures, and for the courage to continue. Our task will never be complete, since we can never reach moral perfection, but when we call out to God, He is there and provides us comfort and assurance.

Jewish prayer reflects the faith that God loves the Jewish people despite our failings and is with us no matter where we may be. God gave us the Torah as a sign of the covenant between us and Him. If we follow it, we will be assured of health, safety, happiness, and eternal life. God will fulfill our aspirations and the hopes of the Jewish people. Many of our prayers express the hope that God will redeem us and lead us back to the Land of Is-

The Shema

The Shema is Judaism's declaration of faith. Loyalty to God and the oneness of God are the two main ideas expressed in this declaration. The Shema also instructs Jews on how to be loyal to this declaration.

All adult Jewish males are required to recite the Shema twice daily. The following is the first paragraph of the Shema, drawn from Deuteronomy 6.

Hear, O Israel! The LORD is our God, The LORD alone. You shall love the LORD your God with all your heart and with all your soul and with all your might. Take to heart these instructions with which I charge you this day. Impress them upon your children. Recite them when you stay at home and when you are away, when you lie down and when you get up. Bind them as a sign on your hand and let them serve as a symbol on your forehead: inscribe them on the doorposts of your house and on your gates.

Tanakh: A New Translation of the Holy Scriptures According to the Traditional Hebrew Text. Philadelphia: Jewish Publication Society, 1985, p. 284.

rael, that He will renew the glory of Israel and allow it to live free in its land, true to God and at peace with its neighbors. We pray for the rebuilding of Jerusalem, the city of our people, as a model of perfect life on earth and the place where God's Presence once dwelt.

Our prayer acknowledges moments of joy and seasons in which we celebrate the life of the Jewish people. God created for us a rich emotional life of joy and gladness, love and relationships, peace and friendship. We take part in all that the world has to offer us and recognize God as the author of the world. When we age, we thank God for the gift of years. When we have children, we thank God for the miracle of birth. When we die, we hope for rest for our souls, freedom from our troubles, reward for our good deeds in life, and comfort for our survivors. We ask God's help in making our hearts open to Him, to Torah, and to other people.

As a sign of His love, God has given us the Sabbath [day of rest; also a sign of the covenant between God and the Israelites] as a special day for rest and spiritual renewal. The Sabbath shows us what a perfect existence might be like and orients us toward a day that is all Sabbath. It is the blueprint for sacred living, when we live focused on the transcendent dimensions of life. It teaches us that redemption is not always in the future but can be had within our own life. It reminds us that the rest of our life is not yet holy and asks us to aspire to reach holiness throughout our life. The greatest gift God can give us, however, is peace within our own heart and within the world. Our prayers recall our striving to view other people kindly, to be modest and fair in all our dealings. We look to a world free of bloodshed and greed. Our thoughts are concentrated on improving ourselves and making the world a better place. . . .

According to Halakhah [the legal system which points out the way of life for the Jewish people], certain prayers can be said only when a prayer quorum (*minyan*) is assembled. The minimum number that defines a congregation is ten adult males. This is based upon Moses' designation of the ten scouts who explored the Land of Israel at his command as a "congregation." Rabbinic legend maintains that the divine Presence dwells in the midst of a congregation of ten men who pray together.

Jewish prayer generally consists of the public recitation of written prayers in the synagogue. All Jewish prayers are written in the first person plural ("we") to emphasize the collective longings of the Jewish people. Despite its public nature, prayer is a solitary act during which each individual prays to God. Written prayers are not spontaneous creations; they are often drawn from biblical sources. But many prayers began as expressions in people's own words or as common and popular versions of particular beliefs. The general framework for prayers existed in the talmudic period but was not fixed as word-for-word formulations until later. Prayers in the talmudic period [when Jewish traditions were accumulated; from around 200 B.C. to A.D. 500] were recited from memory.

The order of the prayers was not fixed until the ninth century, when recognized services were bound together in prayer books called the Siddur, which means "order." The first Siddur was the Seder of Rav Amram Gaon (ca. 850) based on the traditions of Jews living in Babylonia. Subsequent Siddurim (plural) reflecting Babylonian practice were modified in light of other traditions and circulated as the prayer books of German Jewry (*Mahzor Vitry*) and later of Sephardic Kabbalistic Jewry (*Nusah ha-*

An). The first printed prayer books appeared in Europe in 1485, shortly after the printing press was developed.

American Jews utilize prayer books that are published by each modern denomination. Each book includes many of the most common written prayers but adds, removes, or modifies other prayers to express the denomination's own set of beliefs. There are traditional Orthodox prayer books such as Philip Birnbaum's *Daily Prayer Book* (1949) and the Art Scroll Siddur; Conservative prayer books such as *The Sabbath and Festival Prayer Book* (1946) and *Siddur Sim Shalom* (1985); Reconstructionist prayer books such as *Kol Haneshamah* (1989); and Reform versions that include *The Union Prayer Book* (1894–95, 1922, 1940) and the more recent *Gates of Prayer* (1984). . . .

For the rabbis of the talmudic era, the primary purpose of prayer was to educate us in the sacred beliefs of Judaism through regular repetition and reinforcement. This kind of prayer discipline was a Jewish innovation in the ancient world and was adopted by Christianity and Islam later on. Prayers of thanksgiving and praise express the view that there is a divine dimension in all aspects of reality: "The righteous pronounce a blessing over every single matter that they eat, drink, see, or hear." A rabbinic passage indicates: "An evil person is thought of as dead because he sees the sun shine and does not bless God . . . or because he sees the sun set and does not bless God. . . . But the righteous recite blessings upon everything they eat, drink, see, or hear."

Prayers of request convey the idea that we can inspire God to intervene in the course of events. According to rabbinic thinking, God is moved by the prayers of Israel. When Israelites pray, God symbolically "hugs them in His arms, kisses them, remembers their exile, and hastens their redemption." The midrash [commentaries on the Bible made by rabbis and collected over the centuries into a body of literature] explains that the more a person turns to God to answer his needs and wants, the more God loves him.

Prayer was seen as the spiritual dimension of Jewish ritual behavior. The Talmud explains that prayer is "service of the heart," based on the verse "to love the Lord your God and to serve Him with all your heart" (Deuteronomy 11:13). Other passages stress the importance of heartfelt prayer: "A man's prayer is not heard until he makes his heart [soft] like flesh." Prayer was regarded as requiring great mental concentration and effort. One's thoughts should be directed to God: "When you pray, know before Whom you stand." All distractions should be avoided: "Even if a man is greeted by a king while praying, he may not return the greeting. And even if a snake is wound around his heel, he may not interrupt his prayer."

The critical ingredients in rabbinic prayer are intention (*kavanah*) and attentiveness. The personal element of intention is what gives the words of prayer the power to be heard. The most important factor is the concentration on and conviction in the meaning of the words of prayer.

CHAPTER 3

Rites, Rituals, and the Sacredness of Time

Keeping the Sabbath

by Francine Klagsbrun

The Sabbath, the seventh day of the week and a day of rest, is the key observance of the Jewish faith. Jews believe that God, having completed creation, rested on the seventh day. Jews abstain from work to commemorate that event. Keeping the Sabbath is also commandment four out of ten handed down by God to Moses on Mount Sinai. The Sabbath has other implications for Jews. It is a covenant, or agreement, between God and the Israelites and serves as a sign of God's consecration of them. More than being a respite from work and its daily concerns, the Sabbath is a time for being spiritual and reflective of the glory of God's creation.

The commemoration of the Sabbath begins on Friday night about twenty minutes before sundown with the lighting of candles in the home and the reciting of a blessing. Worship services are held in synagogues Friday evening and during the morning, afternoon, and evening of the following day, the Sabbath. Families gather in the late afternoon of the Sabbath to take part in a meal and recite blessings, hymns, and prayers. The Sabbath—a time of joyfulness, relaxation, and closeness with family members and friends—is the culmination of the week.

In the following selection Francine Klagsbrun examines the Sabbath commandment and its appearance in two books of the Bible, Exodus and Deuteronomy. Both

Francine Klagsbrun, *The Fourth Commandment: Remember the Sabbath Day.* New York: Harmony Books, 2002. Copyright © 2002 by Francine Klagsbrun. All rights reserved. Reproduced by permission of Harmony Books, a division of Random House, Inc.

versions of the commandment share basic features: the refraining from work on the seventh day and the extension of the Sabbath rest to all members of a household, including slaves and animals. By refraining from work, Klagsbrun points out, humans imitate God by bringing creative activity to a halt. By doing so they experience that most elusive freedom, the freedom to control time.

Klagsbrun is an author, columnist, and lecturer who writes on social and religious themes. Her books include *Jewish Days: A Book of Jewish Life and Culture Around the Year* and *Voices of Wisdom: Jewish Ideals and Ethics for Everyday Life.*

The Ten Commandments open with the words *your God*, and end with *your neighbor*. The first three concern reverence for God, the last six concern reverence for human life. Fourth in line, the Sabbath command deals with both our relations to God and our relations to one another. In that sense it spans the ideals of all the others; like Jacob's ladder [a vision seen by Jacob, a biblical patriarch of the book of Genesis], it spans heaven and earth. "If in the Ten Commandments is enfolded the whole Torah [the entire body of written and oral law]," the poet Hayim Nahman Bialik once said, "then in the Sabbath are probably enfolded all the Ten Commandments."

The commandments appear as a whole in two biblical books, Exodus and Deuteronomy. In Exodus, seven weeks after fleeing from Egypt, the people of Israel encamp at the foot of Mount Sinai. There, amid thunder and smoke and the piercing blare of a horn, God's commandments ring out from above the mountaintop. The

Shabbat [Hebrew for Sabbath] commandment in Exodus reads:

> Remember the Sabbath day and keep it holy. Six days you shall labor and do all your work, but the seventh day is a Sabbath of the Eternal your God: you shall not do any work—you, your son or daughter, your male or female slave, or your cattle, or the stranger who is within your settlements. For in six days the Eternal made heaven and earth and sea and all that is in them, and rested on the seventh day; therefore the Eternal blessed the Sabbath day and hallowed it.

Almost forty years later, as the Israelites stand poised to enter and conquer Canaan [the Promised Land of the Israelites], Moses recounts to them the events and laws of those years of wandering in the desert. His words, in Deuteronomy, include the Ten Commandments, but with some variations, particularly in the Sabbath command. It reads:

> Observe the Sabbath day and keep it holy, as the Eternal your God has commanded you. Six days you shall labor and do all your work, but the seventh day is a Sabbath of the Eternal your God; you shall not do any work—you, your son or your daughter, your male or female slave, your ox or your ass, or any of your cattle, or the stranger in your settlements, so that your male and female slave may rest as you do. Remember that you were a slave in the land of Egypt and the Eternal your God freed you from there with a mighty hand and an outstretched arm; therefore the Eternal your God has commanded you to observe the Sabbath day.

The two versions of the commandment share basic features. Both make refraining from work on the seventh day of the week a duty that humans owe to God. Both extend the Sabbath rest to all members of a household, including slaves and even animals. . . . In

Shabbat Candle-Lighting Prayer

Setting the Table

The sabbath table should be set with at least two candles (representing the dual commandments to remember and observe the sabbath), a glass of wine, and at least two loaves of challah [a sweet bread served on Shabbat and holidays]. The challah loaves should be whole, and should be covered with a bread cover, towel or napkin.

Lighting Candles

Candles should be lit no later than 18 minutes before sundown. For the precise time when shabbat begins in your area, consult the list of candle lighting times provided by the Orthodox Union or any Jewish calendar.

At least two candles should be lit, representing the dual commandments to remember and to keep the sabbath. The candles are lit by the woman of the household. After lighting, she waves her hands over the candles, welcoming in the sabbath. Then she covers her eyes, so as not to see the candles before reciting the blessing, and recites the blessing. The hands are then removed from the eyes, and she looks at the candles, completing the mitzvah [commandment] of lighting the candles.

Barukh atah Adonai, Elohaynu, melekh ha-olam,
Blessed are You, Lord, our God, King of the Universe,
asher kid' shanu b'mitzvolav, v'tzivanu
who sanctifies us with his commandments, and commands us
l'had'lik neir shel shabbat (Amein)
to light the candles of Shabbat (Amen)

Shabbat Evening Home Ritual, *Judaism 101*. www.jewfaq.org.

both, religious duty is interwoven with humanitarian concerns; humanitarian duty has its source in a religious obligation.

Humans Imitate God

But even more than these similarities, the differences between the two versions of the commandment highlight its essential themes. This is the longest of the commandments and the only one among the ten that gives a rationale for its existence, because unlike the others, the reason for this one is not apparent. Why, after all, does the Bible decree a Sabbath day of rest? The explanation varies in the two texts.

The reason given for the Sabbath commandment in Exodus ties the day's rest to the ordering of the universe. The words of the text—"For in six days the Eternal made heaven and earth . . . "—carry us back to the opening of the Bible, to the first chapters in Genesis. There, day-by-day God creates the world and all that is in it. On the seventh day God stops creating, blesses the day, and declares it holy. By refraining from work on the Sabbath, as the commandment dictates, humans imitate God, what the philosophers call *imitatio Dei*. In celebrating Shabbat each week we also re-create the cosmic order, tuning the cadence of our lives to the pattern of work and rest the Bible tells us existed from the beginning of time.

But what does it mean for God to "rest"? Does the Creator of the universe have human needs for food, drink, and rest? Was creation so difficult that God had to take a break afterward? Early Islamic texts attacked Judaism on just those grounds, accusing Jews of holding an anthropomorphic concept of a deity who, like humans, needed to rest. The Bible critic Moshe Weinfeld suggests that the prophet Isaiah may have been so uncomfortable with the idea of the omnipotent [all-powerful] God of the vast cosmos resting after hard labor that, almost as if to counter it, he dwells on Gods' endurance and infinite strength. "The Lord is God from of old," he proclaims, "Creator of the earth from end to end, / He never grows faint or weary, / His wisdom cannot be fathomed [understood]." The sages may have been so uncomfortable with the concept of God resting the way ordinary mortals do that they explained the biblical description strictly as a lesson. If Scripture can portray the all-powerful God creating the universe in six days and resting on the seventh, they said, how much more do humans, weak as they are, need to rest on the seventh day. . . .

The image of God resting on the seventh day is especially important, forming as it does the basis for so many of the laws and practices of Shabbat. We can get a better understanding of what that image intends by looking again at the language in the Genesis story of creation. The Hebrew there does not literally mean that God rested after creating the world and everything in it, but that God "ceased" from the divine labors on the seventh day. The word *Shabbat* has the same root as the Hebrew verb for ceased. God's "rest" was ceasing, stepping back as it were from creating.

The sages [wise men] put it nicely. After finishing the process of creation, they said, God prevented the world, and particularly the seas, from expanding further by declaring "Enough!" (They interpreted one of the names for God in the Bible, El Shaddai, as "the God who said 'Enough!'"—from the Hebrew word *dai*, which means "enough.") By extension, Shabbat is not simply about relaxing or sleeping. It's about declaring "enough" (or enough already): enough technology, enough building, enough fighting against time. For one day a week, humans cease from creative activity, step back, and, like God, bring their everyday world to a standstill. That is the underlying message of the Sabbath commandment in the book of Exodus, the meaning behind resting as God did on the Sabbath day. . . .

Memorializing Deliverance

No mention of creation or God resting or the blessing the Sabbath received appears in the Shabbat commandment in the book of Deuteronomy. Instead, Moses states: "Remember that you were a slave in the land of Egypt and the Eternal your God freed you from there . . . therefore the Eternal your God has commanded you to observe the Sabbath day." This explanation appears somewhat removed from the day itself, not as closely tied to it as the other. How does God's freeing Israel from Egypt lead to sanctifying the Sabbath?

The answer unfolds in layers. To begin with, the image of God in this version of the commandment matches the image of God in the first commandment, which reads: "I the Eternal am your God who brought you out of the land of Egypt. . . ." This is a familiar God. This is the God who works through history, the God whose liberation of the Israelites from Egypt forms a central theme of the Bible and lies at the core of Jewish life. In addressing the Israelites shortly before his death, Moses is speaking to people who witnessed that liberation or heard about it directly from their parents or other family members. For them, God as creator may seem remote. God as redeemer is the God they know. Calling up that aspect of the divine in the Sabbath commandment stirs in them memories of the slavery they suffered and God's feats in delivering them from it. Observing the Sabbath God ordained is a way of memorializing their deliverance and honoring the deity who brought it about.

But in addressing the Israelites Moses is also addressing generations to come, for as the Passover Haggadah [the text prescribed for the home service on Passover] teaches, every one of us must view ourselves as though we personally came out of Egypt. This version of the Sabbath command brings us, too, closer to the God we know most about, the God who freed our ancestors from oppression, and who stands for justice and liberation.

On one level, then, the Sabbath commandment in Deuteronomy is about remembering the Israelites' slavery and showing gratitude to God for redeeming them and their descendants from it. On a deeper level, it is about translating that memory and redemption into treating others with kindness and generosity, especially those who are weak and vulnerable as the Israelites once were. . . .

In the Sabbath commandment, applying Israel's past history to its current life means giving slaves, servants, and resident aliens a day of rest and serenity each week equal to that enjoyed by the master and mistress of a household. To assure that equality, the commandment in Deuteronomy spells out, "so that your male and female slave may rest as you do." There is no equivocating here. The Sabbath belongs to all members of the household. For those in charge, remembering Egypt transmutes into remembering how it feels to be mistreated and therefore into being vigilant about treating others humanely. I often quote my father's description of how, in his early years of employment, a poor immigrant boy working in the men's clothing industry, workers labored seven days a week without a break. It wasn't until the 1920s and 1930s that the United States enacted labor laws to ease the workers' burdens, and such laws still don't exist in many parts of the world. Yet four thousand years ago, my father would say, the Bible established a day of rest a week for everyone, including the lowliest of servants and the animals they used in their work. . . .

An Affirmation of Freedom

A final layer of meaning in this version of the commandment touches most directly on contemporary life. Simply put: Shabbat affirms our own freedom, not only that of servants and slaves. This may be the most difficult aspect of the Sabbath to assimilate. Freedom? But what about the many restrictions and prohibitions?

The concept of freedom dominates Shabbat despite prohibitions and restrictions, and some might say because of them. The freedom of Shabbat comes from the potential it holds to control time, perhaps the most far-reaching form of freedom anyone can experience. . . .

Oppressed by unrelenting demands, many of us feel incapable of controlling our time. ("Time is my enemy," I lament as deadlines and obligations crush down on me.) Shabbat offers such control. It offers a day when instead of fighting time, we may luxuriate in it. Instead of feeling chained to routine, we may break loose and breathe freely. One of the Hebrew words the Torah uses in connection with the Sabbath rest for both God and humans is *va'yinnafash*, which generally means to be refreshed or restored, but literally has within it the root of the word *nefesh*, or "soul." A medieval mystic explained that when God gave the world the Sabbath, God gave the world its soul.

The Feast of Passover

by Ira Steingroot

Passover, or Pesach, is one of the most important Jewish celebrations of the year. Its focal point is the seder, a ritual meal that commemorates the escape of the Israelites from slavery in Egypt, an event described in the book of Exodus in the Bible. Coming as it does during spring, Passover also celebrates rebirth, renewal, and a new beginning. During the Passover seder, family and friends gather at the table and hear the story of how the Israelites began their journey out of Egypt, a trip that would bring them to Mt. Sinai and the handing down of the Ten Commandments by God to Moses.

The book containing all the texts and directions for the Passover seder is called the Haggadah. Each person at the Passover seder has a copy so he or she can follow the evening's prayers and recitations. At the Passover seder, the story of the physical and spiritual redemption of the Israelites is transmitted from parents to their children. The youngest child at the table is required to ask four questions, beginning with "Why is this night different from all other nights?" An adult responds with an explanation, thereby fulfilling the instruction to tell the Exodus story to the next generation. Observant Jews use the recollection of the liberation from slavery as a way to focus on their own spiritual redemption.

The details of the first part of the Passover seder are

Ira Steingroot, *Keeping Passover: Everything You Need to Know to Bring the Ancient Tradition to Life and Create Your Own Passover Celebration.* San Francisco: HarperSanFrancisco, 1995. Copyright © 1995 by Ira Steingroot. All rights reserved. Reproduced by permission of HarperCollins Publishers.

contained in the following selection by Ira Steingroot, a writer based in Berkeley, California. In providing extensive background on the Haggadah, Steingroot's goal is to help Jews derive the most meaning from their seder.

What could be more Jewish than a meal that cannot be eaten without a book? Perhaps this is just a clever way to get to read at the dinner table. The Haggadah is the book containing all the texts and ritual directions for the Passover seder. Pieced together with bits of Tanakh [Bible], *siddur* [prayer book], Mishnah [oral law], Talmud [body of Jewish tradition], midrash [commentary], medieval *piyyutim* (liturgical poems), and folk song, it is a collage of 4,000 years of Jewish life, thought, and literature. It is our ancient *grimoire*, a grammar of the seder's magical rites, casting spells, enchanting, and calling down curses. Yet it goes beyond the magic of revenge, desire, and prophylaxis [something taken to preserve health]. It is through this variegated [varied] text that the protective magic of the mute book is elevated to a higher level of personal communal transformation.

If the parts of the Haggadah seem disconnected from one another, it may be because this book is actually the surviving fragments of an anthology on the subject of Passover chosen over the last 3,300 years. The originals may have made more sense, but our people culled out of them whatever was not poetry. The dull prose that made it all cohere was jettisoned along the way. Only those bits and pieces that were green and alive, that spoke to the heart, were kept in the final work, which is never truly finished. . . .

Overture to the Seder

Now we will go back over what we have already brought to the seder table and see how it meshes with the Haggadah text. The passages will be referred to by their Hebrew and Aramaic tag lines or with extracts in English. As with the *berakhot* [blessings; singular: *berakhah*] the more Hebrew you can comfortably add to the recitation, the more powerful are the tools you have at your disposal for breaking through to "what is this service to you," a heightened sense of the moment, the holy. . . .

Ritual action 1: Search the house for chametz [leavened grain products]. This is a good place to mention that besides the berakhah said before the *bedikat chametz*, the following is said in Aramaic after the search:

> All leaven in my possession which I have not seen and have not removed and of which I am not aware is hereby nullified and ownerless as the dust of the earth.

Ritual action 2: Burn the chametz. By nine or ten o'clock on the morning before the seder, *erev* Pesach (the day preceding Passover), we should have eaten the last *chametzdikhe* food [anything made with leavened grain] we had set aside. After that, we burn all the chametz turned up in our search the night before and say the following variation of the above statement:

> All leaven in my possession which I have seen or not seen, which I have removed or not removed, is hereby nullified and ownerless as the dust of the earth. . . .

Ritual action 3: Light the candles. Berakhot over the lighting of candles followed by the blessing of the children. At this point we can add the table of contents to our seder, Kadesh Urchatz, the recitation or chanting of the fifteen prescribed steps of the ceremony. . . .

Up to this point, all we have done is prelude or over-ture to the seder proper, which is now ready to begin.

The First Five Steps

Step I. Kadesh [sanctification]

Ritual action 4: Pour the first cup of wine. . . . This Kadesh can involve up to five berakhot. Throughout the ceremony, whenever we lift the wine cup or drink the wine, the matzot [unleavened bread] are covered. The matzot are slightly uncovered the rest of the time.

Step II. Urchatz [washing]

Ritual action 5: Wash hands, Urchatz, by pouring wa-ter over them from a pitcher.

Step III. Karpas [vegetable]

Ritual action 6: Eat the green vegetable [a symbol of the modest beginnings of the Jewish people] dipped in saltwater [a symbol of tears shed as a result of slavery]. Everyone dips the karpas and eats, either leaning to the left or sitting upright, after reciting the berakhot.

Step IV. Yachatz [dividing]

Ritual action 7: Break the middle matzo and set aside the afikoman [matzo to be eaten at the end of the meal]. The middle matzo of the three is divided, Yachatz, in half. One half is wrapped up either to be stolen from the leader of the seder by the children or hidden from the children by the leader. We have had wine, an appetizer, and broken our bread, but we do not eat. We have done quite a number of mystifying procedures and by now everyone should be eager to find out why.

Step V. Maggid [telling the story]

Ritual action 8: Display the matzo and the seder plate

A Jewish family celebrates Passover, a holiday that commemorates the Jews' liberation from slavery in Egypt.

[a special plate with sections for each food eaten or having symbolic importance]. The seder plate and matzot are lifted up and displayed. Alternatively, the seder plate is removed or put at the opposite end of the table temporarily, and the remaining two-and-a-half matzot are lifted up and displayed. Some remove only the shankbone and egg [other symbolic foods on the seder plate] during the display of the matzot, especially if the matzot are on or within the seder plate. Other alternatives are to lift only the seder plate or only the matzot.

The Haggadah Text

Text a: We have finally come to our Haggadah text, the Maggid, the actual "Telling," from the same root as Haggadah. We explain what we are doing, why we display the matzot and seder plate symbols, with the Aramaic words, *Ha lachma anya*. These words refer to eating the Passover sacrifice as well as being in exile, inconsistencies that make it impossible to date this passage with certainty. Some people have the custom of opening the door while this is being said:

> This is the bread of affliction which our ancestors
> ate in the land of Egypt.
> Let all who are hungry enter and eat, let all who
> are needy enter to share our Passover.
> This year here, next year in Israel.
> This year as slaves, next year in freedom.

Notice the parallel construction of the sentences, common throughout Jewish literature, especially in the Bible. The sages of the Talmud made a pun out of the words *lechem oni*, "the bread of poverty," and read it as *onin*, making this key phrase mean "the bread over which many words are spoken."

Why Aramaic? A folk belief has it that demons can only understand Hebrew, so we avoid the possibility of inviting them by phrasing the invitation in Aramaic. Beyond that, Aramaic was the language of our exile in Babylonia in the sixth century B.C., and continued to be the Jewish vernacular until the ninth century A.D. . . .

In using it we remind ourselves of the repetition of our exile, the paradigm of Jewish experience. We also remind ourselves of key transitional moments in our lives: marriage, divorce, death, holidays, and bar mitzvah (*bar*, son, is Aramaic). We associate it with the important Jewish metaphysical activities of study, Talmud, and mysticism, *Zohar*. Aramaic was the language of the common people, of the poor, like the poor bread (ha-lachma anya) we display at this point. It was a language whose inviting words would have been understood by all. It reminds us that once we were all slaves.

*By the rivers of Babylon, there we sat down, yea, we
wept, when we remembered Zion. . . . For there they that
carried us away captive required of us a song. . . . How
shall we sing the Lord's song in a strange land?*
                                        —Psalm 137:1, 3–4

Each successive year of exile has required that we answer that last question anew to our own satisfaction. . . .

As we will see, the whole story of the Jewish people
from Abraham on is encompassed in the Haggadah
narrative. Following the forty years of wandering, entry
into Canaan, and building of the Temple [center of
worship in Jerusalem], we have the phase where we
have been redeemed and we have our own land. Then
the story leans more toward total joy, with only the
slightest mingling of melancholy about our past and
dread of the wild forces of the universe.

The catastrophe of the Babylonian captivity gives the
Haggadah a whole new meaning. Now we had a ceremony and story ready-made to explain this crisis.
Again, the exile ended and there was a return to the
Holy Land. A new Temple was built and sacrifices began
again. Neither of these Temple periods was insignificant. Each went on about 500 years. That is roughly a
millennia of Passovers reenacting the Exodus paschal
sacrifice. Further catastrophes occurred, including the
final destruction of the Temple and banishment from
the Holy Land [in A.D. 70], and they were added on to
the book and the ceremony, but always within the context of the Babylonian exile.

Ritual action 9: Pour the second cup of wine. During
the breaking in half of the afikoman and the mention-
ing of the bread of affliction, the wine cup was empty.
As we move toward our next toast, we refill the cup. It
will take a long time until we drink this cup, but

throughout this Maggid section the wine cup will have many featured moments. There is a certain comicality in our constant movement toward drinking the wine and the equally constant way that the Haggadah pulls the cup away from us. We recited the Kiddush [sanctification] over the first cup of wine. With the cup empty, we display the matzo, beginning the Maggid. Now we recite the rest of the Maggid over this second cup of wine.

The Four Questions

Text b: Following our argument or abstract, the invitation and general statement of what we are doing, comes the most famous text of the Haggadah, the *fier kashes* (four questions or perplexities), from which this chapter takes its title: *Mah-Nishtannah Ha-layleh Hazeh mi-kol ha-laylot.* This is usually translated as "Why is this night different from all other nights?" or "What is different about this night from all other nights?" It could also be rendered, "How different this night is from all other nights!" Originally, the leader asked the questions, but since the later Middle Ages the youngest child has become the traditional catechist. Not only are the unusual actions of the evening being questioned, but also why this evening merits this distinction. It is through the questions of the youngest that the rest of us are instructed.

The questions, or amplification of the first question, continue with:

1. For on all other nights we eat leavened or unleavened bread, on this night only unleavened.
2. For on all other nights we eat all kinds of herbs, on this night only bitter.

3. For on all other nights we are not obligated to dip
even one time, on this night we dip two times.

For on all other nights we eat either sitting up or re-
clining, on this night we all recline. . . .

These questions were originally asked after the meal,
when they would have made more sense. The questions and the Maggid were moved ahead of the meal so
that the children would be awake to hear the story.
When they were moved to the beginning of the seder,
along with the rest of the Maggid, they became quizzi-
cal in themselves. Their function now is to generate the
remainder of the Maggid section of the Haggadah.
These specific questions are not needed to kick off the
answers. Any question will do to generate the "Funny
you should mention that" response. In fact, they are
never directly answered in the Haggadah at all, although we can piece together the answers from the ensuing reply. They represent the types of questions that
we might ask, or could ask, or should ask. They prime
the question pump.

Once We Were Slaves

Text c: The general answer to all these questions and to
everything else odd about tonight is that Avadim Hay-
inu, Once we were slaves:

> Once we were slaves to Pharaoh in Egypt, and the
> Lord our God brought us forth from there with a
> mighty hand and an outstretched arm. And if the
> Holy One had not brought our ancestors forth from
> Egypt, then we and our children and our children's
> children would still be slaves to Pharaoh in Egypt.
> And even if all of us were wise, all of us full of under-
> standing, all of us elders, all of us full of knowledge of
> the Torah, we would still be obligated to perform the

mitzvah [commandment] of recounting the story of
the departure from Egypt. And the more one elaborates upon the departure from Egypt, the more praise-
worthy one is.

Here, in a passage usually read in unison by the whole
company, we see some key themes developing. The
Mishnah requires that the Haggadah begin in shame,
our slavery, and end in glory, our redemption. Our liberation was not something done once and no longer relevant, but affects us to this day. No matter how old we are
or how much we know, we must tell the story anew
every year. Indeed, the more we tell, the better it is. . . .

[The seder continues with the following steps: a second washing of hands, blessings over grain products
and matzo, eating of bitter herbs and apples, nuts, and
cinnamon, the festive dinner, the search for the last
piece of matzo and a grace after the meal.]

Living Kosher

by Joseph Grunblatt

Kosher is a Hebrew word meaning "fit" or "proper." Its most common usage is in reference to foods that are declared fit and proper to eat in accordance with Jewish dietary practices called kashruth. The Bible describes the animals that are permitted to be eaten (for example, those that chew the cud and have split hooves, such as sheep and cattle) and those that are not (for example, pigs and camels) and also prescribes the manner in which animals should be slaughtered. Dietary laws also pertain to the correct preparation of food. Certain foods, such as meat and milk, are rigorously separated according to the biblical command: "Thou shall not cook a kid (baby goat) in its mother's milk." To prevent cross-contamination, kosher homes will have separate cooking pots and pans and separate plates and utensils for use with meat and another set of the same for use with milk products.

While some Jews may not follow strict dietary laws, others find it important to do so in order to maintain their Jewish identity. There are other reasons for keeping kosher. In following laws about what foods may or may not be eaten observant Jews attempt to impart discipline and a strict morality to their everyday lives. Keeping kosher is less difficult today than it was years ago. Most supermarkets carry a wide variety of kosher foods, airlines carry kosher meals, and travelers are able to find kosher restaurants and food stores while away from home. Finally, many non-Jews in the United States are unaware that the mass-produced foods they eat have been declared kosher by the Orthodox Union, or OU, the organization responsible for certifying kosher products and trademarking them with the symbol of an uppercase U inside an O.

In the following selection, Rabbi Joseph Grunblatt of the Queens Jewish Center in Forest Hills, New York, describes the meaning of the term *kosher* and the meaning of the law behind it. Grunblatt points out that kashruth is a living reality for many Jews. In addition to being vice chairman of the NCSY National Youth Commission, Grunblatt is the author of *Exile and Redemption: Meditations on Jewish History.*

The word "kosher" is one of Judaism's contributions to the international vocabulary. People of other cultures and languages use the term in its original meaning—denoting that which is proper and meets accepted rules and standards.

In Judaism, the term "kosher" is not used exclusively for ritually edible food. We refer to tefillin [the boxlike accessory worn on the head and on the left arm by adult males during prayer] and Torah scrolls [the scrolls, mounted on rollers and kept in the sanctuary of the synagogue, containing the first five books of the Hebrew Bible] as kosher to mean that they meet all halachic (Jewish legal) requirements. The expression can even be applied to people. Acceptable witnesses are called edim k'sherim; adam kasher is an upright, proper, observant Torah Jew. Its most common use today, of course, is in regard to food. Food is relevant to all, and it is regarding food that "kosher" or "non-kosher" is encountered most often.

Food may be designated non-kosher for a variety of reasons. They include the species involved (for example, the pig); the manner in which the food was processed (such as an animal improperly slaughtered, or the mixing of milk and meat); or time (leavened product [one made with a grain that will rise when mixed with water] not properly disposed of prior to Passover or food cooked on the Sabbath).

A Unique Lifestyle

Many an observant Jew has been asked by a skeptic at one time or another. "Do you really think God cares what we eat?" What the person is actually asking is; "Do you really think God cares?" Philosophers from Aristotle [Greek philosopher who lived from 384 to 322 B.C.] to Hegel [German philosopher who lived from 1770 to 1831] have argued that God can only be concerned with universals, not with particulars—not even human beings.

But the God of Abraham, Isaac and Jacob does care about every individual. In the words of the Psalmist: "And His mercy extends to all of His creatures." To us, He is "Our Father in Heaven." A father cares about the moral and spiritual development of his child but also takes care that the child is properly fed. In fact, the two are related. Good nutrition makes learning and every other form of spiritual and physical training easier.

We do not mean to imply that the kashrut laws are nutritional and hygienic regulations, even though that claim has been made. We would be hard put to prove that kashrut observance makes for better health, and conversely, living non-kosher creates greater hazards for our physical well-being. Besides, we do not look upon the Torah as an ancient book of science, but rather as an ever-new and eternally fresh source of religious truth and practice. It does make sense, though, to argue that, as our creator, God knows what we require to conduct our lives as dedicated and spiritually-oriented Jews. 613 commandments to make the total Jew and kashrut is certainly a substantial component.

Some who have dabbled in the art of explaining mitsvos (commandments) have suggested a number of plausible interpretations for the overall structure of kashrut. Some writers emphasize the disciplinary aspects of the kashrut regulations—and rightfully so. So much of Torah is disciplinary in nature and self-discipline is vital in one's religious life. Kashrut undoubtedly projects sensitivity towards animals and plants. Therefore, a respect for God's creation, and due humility and thoughtfulness compels one to rely upon lower forms of existence for sustenance.

Others have emphasized the by-products of kashrut. Skirting the inner meaning of the law, they focus on its impact on Jewish living and Jewish survival. Unquestionably, there is a lot of truth to that contention. Living kosher is living like a Jew. It makes one's whole lifestyle unique and distinctive vis-a-vis the outside world. Kashrut surely is a bulwark [protection] against assimilation [absorption into a larger culture].

I would like to add a different concept suggested by our Talmudic sages [scholars who study and comment on the entire body of Jewish tradition]. When speaking of forbidden species, the Torah uses the word tameh (ritually impure or unclean). They note the similarity to another word containing the same root letters: timtum, meaning clogging or blocking. The sages comment that the nature of tum'ah is shemetamtem es halev—it blocks . . . it petrifies the heart. As modern medicine discovers ever-closer relationships between the body and the mind, the idea that what we eat somehow affects what we are spiritually does not ring so mystical anymore.

Samson Raphael Hirsh, the great modern interpreter of Torah Judaism, explains that the massive complex of mitzvos is designed to make the Jew capable of, and sensitive to, his spiritual task. Indeed, the Jewish record for endurance, spiritual creativity and God-centeredness is unparalleled.

A Living Reality

Gone are the days of the local shochet (ritual slaughterer), cheese manufacturer and bakery. Food has become industrialized big business. Mass production and national and international distribution bring new pressures of profit, production, speed, ingredient complexity and product diversification. Now, more than ever, expert supervision is needed to provide the consumer with reliable kashrut certification.

The Ⓤ insignia of the Orthodox Union is a symbol of such expertise and integrity. As a non-profit service organization, the Orthodox Union has been the leader in the field of reliable kashrut for nearly three-quarters of a century. It has made reliable kashrut available in a range of products spanning the gamut of human needs. It has made these products accessible around the world.

But the success story of modern, high-level kashrut

supervision has implications beyond its immediate ac-complishments. It is a theological statement, a testi-mony that Torah is not an "ancient religion essentially geared to an agricultural society," but a living reality that is meaningful and workable in any stage of civi-lization to which ingenuity and technological progress may carry us.

Bar and Bat Mitzvah

by Linda Burghardt

Bar or bat mitzvah (meaning son or daughter of the commandment) is a major event in the life of a Jewish boy or girl. By turning thirteen and twelve, respectively, Jewish boys and girls are regarded as both able *and* obligated to fulfill the precepts of Judaism. They gain the religious privileges afforded to them by their community of fellow believers and also bear responsibility for their actions. Upon reaching the age of thirteen a boy (in some congregations, girls also) can be counted in the number of adult males needed to worship together or hold religious ceremonies.

The idea of a ceremony surrounding bar or bat mitzvah dates from about the fourteenth century. The ceremony involved the boy's reading from the Torah scroll, recitation of a blessing, and chanting. Over the years the ceremonial rite became more elaborate and, in 1922, included girls for the first time. All branches of Judaism—Orthodox, Reform, and Conservative—hold ceremonies to mark bar and bat mitzvah but only after the boy or girl has completed several years of religious education. Today the bar or bat mitzvah ceremony usually takes place at the Sabbath morning service.

Author Linda Burghardt describes the ceremony in the following excerpt from *The Bar and Bat Mitzvah*

Linda Burghardt, *The Bar and Bat Mitzvah Book*. New York: Citadel Press Books, 2004. Copyright © 2004 by Linda Burghardt. All rights reserved. Reproduced by permission of Kensington Publishing Corp. www.kensingtonbooks.com.

Book. Her audience is the secular parent or parents who may not be fully knowledgeable about the ritual and its meaning. Linda Burghardt is a journalist whose articles have appeared in the *New York Times*, the *Chicago Tribune*, and *Jewish World*.

Although the service is the heart of the bar and bat mitzvah, it is without a doubt the least understood part of the entire experience. Many parents begin to plan the event with only a fuzzy idea of what the service consists of and how it is put together, and simply trust the rabbi and cantor [the person who chants/sings the liturgy in the synagogue] to plan it, execute it, and tell them what to do, without ever asking for explanations or finding out if they have any say.

While this system works well enough, active participation is guaranteed to increase the enjoyment and the meaning of the day. The larger your role in the service—especially in the planning stages, when you can make choices, decide to add or eliminate optional parts, and help direct the action—the more likely it is that your memories of the day will be as bright as possible.

The Essence of the Ceremony

The first step in taking an active part in the service is to understand exactly what happens. While this will vary somewhat based on the branch of Judaism and the specific rites and rituals honored at your synagogue, the basic structure of the Saturday morning service is the same everywhere. According to Talmudic legend [the Talmud is the body of Jewish tradition], we are each given an extra soul on Shabbat [the Sabbath] with which to enjoy the experience.

The essence of the bar and bat mitzvah ceremony, embedded within the service, is always basically the same. The child is called to the Torah [the first five books of the Bible], recites the blessings, reads a portion from the scroll, then recites the Haftarah blessings [Haftarah is a reading from the other books of the Bible] and chants the reading. Friends and relatives are called up to the bimah [the pedestal on which the Torah scrolls are placed when they are being read] to recite additional blessings and perform various duties, like opening the ark [the chest where the Torah scrolls are kept] and dressing the Torah.

The bar or bat mitzvah child leads parts of the service, delivers a short speech on the meaning of the Torah portion, the d'var Torah, and receives blessings from the rabbi. When the service is over, the family proceeds to the kiddush where blessings are said over

A young Jewish boy reads from the Torah at his bar mitzvah.

the challah [a sweet bread] and the wine, and then to the reception to celebrate.

Attendees at the service will each have a Torah in book form at each seat, along with a Shabbat prayer book, a *siddur*, written in both Hebrew and English. During the service the rabbi will signal whether prayers should be said standing or sitting, aloud or silently, and lead the congregation in responsive readings, while the cantor will chant the prayers and lead the singing.

The service is all about hope, and embodies our wishes and dreams for universal freedom and peace. It begins with the opening prayers, which include psalms from the Bible, songs and meditations, blessings and finally the Barechu, also known as the call to worship.

All congregations begin formal worship with the Shema, the central prayer in Judaism and one of its oldest and most significant, which affirms our belief in one God and contains the central statement of Jewish faith: "Hear, O Israel, Adonai is our God, Adonai is one! Blessed is the glorious realm of God forever and ever."

Next comes the Amidah, sometimes called Tefillah, which means, literally, prayer, and contains seven blessings of praise and gratitude. This prayer, designed to link us to our ancestors, is so important we stand to recite it. Its purpose is to help us create a sacred space within ourselves through which we can each address God in our own personal way.

This is followed by the Torah service, in which the Torah is taken from the holy ark. It is during this part of the service that the bar or bat mitzvah child will ascend the bimah, chant or recite the Torah and Haftarah portions, and deliver the d'var Torah.

The service concludes with several prayers, including

the Aleinu, which asks us to remain true to our Jewish identity, and the Mourner's Kaddish, said in honor of the deceased, and ends with a closing hymn and benediction.

Inside the Synagogue

Becoming familiar with the sanctuary where the service will take place can make you feel more at ease and in control during the bar or bat mitzvah ceremony. It is a good idea to spend as much time as you can looking around ahead of time, examining the ritual objects, getting to know what everything is called and studying the architecture.

All synagogues contain a light, called the *ner tamid*, which is always kept burning. This eternal light is placed above the holy ark, the sacred storage area where the Torah scrolls are kept. Some arks contain one Torah scroll, some two, and others several. *Torah* literally means "teaching" or "instruction."

Yad

Near the Torah will be a pointer, called a *yad*, which means "hand" in Hebrew. Yads are used by Torah readers to point to letters and words in the scroll so that the oils in our hands and fingers never come in contact with the parchment and risk soiling or spotting it. Yads are usually made of silver. The tip or pointer is shaped like an actual tiny hand with the index finger extended and is attached to the end of a foot-long stick.

You will probably also see a seven-branched *menorah* or candelabra, usually made of silver, which symbolizes the seven days of Creation. The synagogue will also have silver candlesticks and a kiddush cup to use on Friday evenings to bless the wine and welcome Shabbat.

At the front of the sanctuary is the *bimah*, the raised platform from which the prayers are led and the Torah is read. *Bimah* literally means "stage." Up on the bimah will be a pulpit from which the rabbi gives sermons, and also a smaller podium or lectern for the cantor. The seats in the sanctuary are arranged in rows or semicircles, or sometimes in a large square. Ritual items in the synagogue include the *tallitim*, or prayer shawls, and *kippot*, or head coverings, also called *yarmulkes*.

Handing Down the Torah

A very beautiful and moving part of the Shabbat service begins when the Torah is taken from the ark and handed down, literally, from one generation to the next. With the bar or bat mitzvah child already on the bimah, the parents are called up, along with the grandparents, and the rabbi hands the oldest family member the Torah.

If you have never held a Torah in your arms, it is a transcendent experience. Its volume and heft symbolize the weighty information it contains, and as the grandparents pass it to the parents who pass it to the child, the sense that the teachings of our tradition are being passed on within the family is felt physically and becomes very real.

Sometimes siblings and older members of the congregation are also invited to participate in this ceremony of continuity, as the family stands together on the bimah, publicly asserting their love and respect for Jewish teachings, showing real, material proof that Judaism is being transmitted to the next generation.

This ceremony, silent and deeply moving, is an acknowledgment of all the child's work in getting to this point. It is in this moment, more than any other in the service, that the congregation senses that the child has been accepted into the chain of tradition.

Many bar and bat mitzvah families have said that they sensed the presence of deceased family members during the passing of the Torah, as its sacred teachings and ancient blessings moved from hand to hand and heart to heart. Although grandparents' and great-grandparents' lives are over, families often feel for the first time how the legacy of their strength to continue their Jewish faith in the face of adversity lives on. This blessing of the spirit is one of the highlights of the Torah service.

When the bar or bat mitzvah child is given the Torah to hold, a procession around the sanctuary begins, with the child in front and the rest of the family following. Often it also includes the rabbi, cantor, and all the other students. Children love this part of the service. They get to move around and relieve some tension, and while congregants reach out and kiss the Torah as it passes, smiling with happiness, children can't help but feel the joy being shared with their family.

When the Torah is brought back to the bimah, it is ceremoniously undressed and unrolled to the portion of the week. Now is the time for the bar or bat mitzvah child to show the work and dedication that went into the study sessions and demonstrate all that has been learned. Some children read a few lines, others several sections, while still others read long portions, depending on the customs of the synagogue and the ability of the student.

In addition to reading from the Torah, most bar and bat mitzvah students also read a portion from the Haftarah. While the Torah is sequential, starting with Creation and ending with the death of Moses, the Haftarah passages are selected for their relationship to the Torah

Confirmation in Judaism

Confirmation is a practice devised by the early Reform movement, originally designed to supplant the *bar mitzvah* ceremony. First introduced by one of the movement's pioneers, Rabbi Israel Jacobson, in his German congregation in 1810, it originally bore more than a faint resemblance to German Protestant rites of passage. *Bar mitzvah* proved a hardier ritual than the early Reformers had realized, gradually enjoying a resurgence in Reform congregations until, today, it is the more important event of the two.

The difference between *bar mitzvah* and confirmation is more than just the difference between a thirteen-year-old boy or girl and a high school student. *Bar mitzvah* is a celebration of individual achievement and a family affair; but it also marks the recognition of a passage that is not chosen. Confirmation is a celebration of and by the community, a group ceremony whose primary content is intellectual and spiritual, marking an acceptance and affirmation of one's Jewishness.

The Confirmation ceremony takes place as part of the Shavuot [a festival celebrating the giving of the Torah and the harvest of the first fruits] service. The confirmands in a Conservative congregation are called *b'nei Torah* and *b'not Torah*, sons and daughters of the Torah. There is no set liturgy for this event, but the young men and women are encouraged to participate actively in the planning and performance of the festival service as a mark of their commitment to Judaism.

George Robinson, *Essential Judaism: A Complete Guide to Beliefs, Customs, and Rituals.* New York: Pocket Books, 2000, p. 159.

reading. Some readings are prophetic, others are historical, but all are connected to the Torah text in theme.

Haftarah Evokes Torah

There are historical reasons that explain why bar and bat mitzvah children read from both the Torah and the Haftarah. When the Syrian-Greeks conquered the Jewish people in 165 B.C., our ancestors were forbidden to study Torah. In order to keep the traditions alive, they devised a system of correlating each Torah portion with a section from the later biblical writings contained in the Haftarah. Since they were linked thematically, reading the Haftarah evoked the Torah. Thus they outsmarted the rulers' injunction not to study Torah.

Years later, when the Jews regained their freedom and were once again permitted to read from the Torah, they kept the Haftarah in the service because they had grown to love it. Today it enriches the service by providing an extra look at the significance of the Torah portion from another viewpoint.

Haftarah literally means "conclusion" The readings come from the books of the Hebrew Bible called the *Neviim* (Prophets) and *Ketuvim* (Writings) and conclude each Sabbath or holiday Torah reading. They contain many well-known Jewish stories and fables and particularly embody a wealth of Jewish visions.

The Young Person Speaks

It is traditional for bar and bat mitzvah children to give a short speech or sermonette after the Torah and Haftarah readings are over. Called the *d'var Torah*, it literally means the "word of Torah" and is most commonly a commentary on the Torah portion just read. Some-times it is called a *drash*, which is a Hebrew word that means to "uncover" or "expose."

The d'var Torah is a very important part of the service, one many congregants consider a highlight, as it expresses the young person's views and gives listeners the chance to get to know him or her, offering fresh insights and new ways to embrace old truths. Writing and presenting the speech offers the bar and bat mitzvah child a chance to personalize the Torah portion. . . .

To create an interesting d'var Torah takes some planning and thought. To start, bar and bat mitzvah candidates should first study the Torah portion well enough to understand its purpose and outline the salient points. Then they should write a short explanation of what the passages mean and think about how to relate them to real life.

Next, it is a good idea to consult the traditional commentaries and see what our rabbinic scholars have had to say about it down through the ages, then distill their wisdom and decide which parts seem most relevant.

Students can then apply the Torah's teachings to their own lives. Because each child's life is unique, the results are always original and fresh, offering welcome stimulation to congregants interested in learning major lessons through the voice of a young person.

Including Others

One of the joys of the bar and bat mitzvah event is having the opportunity to involve several important people in the service by asking them to chant or recite the blessings before and after each Torah section is read.

This great honor, usually reserved for family members and close friends, is called an *aliyah*, which literally means "going up" in Hebrew, as you are called up to the bimah to read from the Torah. In ancient times, the Torah was read in public from a raised platform, giving rise to the concept of ascending to the Torah. Interestingly, it is also the expression used today when a Jew immigrates to Israel, which is perceived as a spiritual uplifting.

Any Jewish adult may recite or chant the blessings, and this includes your child's friends who have already had their bar or bat mitzvah. They are usually called up to the Torah by their Hebrew names. All congregations will provide a transliterated text, so no one has to read directly from the Hebrew if that is too difficult. However, it is wise to send copies of the blessings well in advance to those to whom you assign an aliyah so they can practice at home before the service. You can ask if they want a printed copy, a tape recording, or both. . . .

The number of blessings you get to assign depends on the day of the week, whether it is a holiday and the synagogue's tradition. At a typical Shabbat service there are seven. It is customary for parents to have the last aliyah before the bar or bat mitzvah child's, leaving you five to assign.

Make sure you tell the people you have assigned which one they have so they know when they will be called. Tell them to sit where they can comfortably get out to go to the bimah when they are called, and remind them to listen for their Hebrew name. If you don't already know the blessings yourself, your child will enjoy teaching them to you so you will be prepared when you are called for your turn.

Performing Honors

In addition to choosing people for an aliyah, you will also be asked whom you would like to have perform the honors. An honor is different from an aliyah because it is a nonspeaking role, and the rules about who can do them are less stringent. For example, most synagogues that will not allow non-Jews to chant the Torah blessings will allow them to perform honors.

After the Torah reading, two people will be called to the bimah, one to hold up the scroll in front of the congregation, the other to dress it after it has been rolled closed. These are honors of great distinction. In addition, honored participants can be asked to open and close the ark and undress the Torah before it is read. . . .

Presenting the Prayer Shawl

There is great variation among synagogues as to how much parents can be involved in the service. If this is important to you, speak to the rabbi early on, find out what is customary and make it known that you want to be an integral part of the service. The benefits of participation are numerous and long-lasting, so do as much as you can.

Most of the time, parents are permitted to ascend the bimah and present their child with a tallit, the prayer shawl that has been used in synagogue worship for thousands of years. This usually occurs at the beginning of the service and is always a very memorable moment.

The word *tallit* comes from the Aramaic and means "to cover." The great Jewish philosopher Maimonides emphasized that the tallit should be worn during prayer, and because of this it is never worn outside the synagogue. It is traditionally worn only in the daytime.

Parents who present the tallit often give a short speech about it, holding it up for the congregation to see and telling about the hopes and dreams it embodies. They might talk about what is unique about the tallit—that it was purchased in Israel, passed down to this generation from the last one, or handmade by a skilled Jewish craftsperson or family member.

Often the tallit will have a blessing stitched into the collar, and you may talk about this too, or you may explain that the ritual fringes, or tzitzit, of the tallit are tied into 613 knots, the number of mitzvot [commandments] the bar or bat mitzvah child will now be obligated to perform.

Very often, parents feel the desire to say a few words of praise for their child as they drape the tallit around his or her shoulders. This can be one of the most moving moments of the service, a time when the love of the parents is made real by the yards of cloth in which they wrap their child.

The bar or bat mitzvah child then says a short blessing: "Blessed are you, Adonai, ruler of the universe, who has sanctified us with your commandments and commanded to wrap ourselves in tzitzit," and ascends the bimah to begin the service.

Most congregations allow parents to say a personal prayer or give a short speech that allows them to express their own feelings toward their child and their sense of gratitude after the Torah service is concluded.

Often this begins with the Shehecheyanu, the short prayer that thanks God for allowing them to reach this day. Sometimes the synagogue wants the talk to be Torah-inspired, and the parents are asked to draw parallels between the portion just read and some personal aspects about their child. But mostly the speech praises the child and provides words of promise for the future that has yet to arrive.

CHAPTER 4

Interpreting, Preserving, and Evolving

The Rabbi as Necessary Teacher

by George Robinson

Unlike Christianity, Judaism (and Islam) does not require the participation of clergy in communal prayer. Jews do not need a priest or a pastor to lead them in speaking to God. In Judaism, only ten adult males (in most congregations, females also) are required to form a minyan, or quorum, for the purpose of prayer. They can also hold a service in any place they believe appropriate. The place could be a synagogue or someone's home. In addition, any Jew over the age of thirteen (for a boy) or twelve (for a girl) can lead a service, read passages from the Torah (the first five books of the Bible), and deliver a sermon. What role then does the rabbi play within the life of the Jewish community?

Rabbi is a word that means "my master" and is the title of a qualified religious authority and teacher. In ancient times *rabbi* was used as a term of respect and identified those individuals who were acknowledged to be experts in Jewish law. At first, rabbis volunteered their knowledge whenever they were asked and earned their living like everyone else—by working at a profession or trade. As they devoted themselves solely to religious matters, however, rabbis began to be paid a salary by the community in which they lived. Today there are

George Robinson, *Essential Judaism: A Complete Guide to Beliefs, Customs, and Rituals.* New York: Pocket Books, 2000. Copyright © 2000 by George Robinson. All rights reserved. Reproduced by permission of Atria, an imprint of Simon & Schuster Adult Publishing Group.

rabbinical seminaries where individuals train to become rabbis in their specific branch of Judaism: Orthodox, Conservative, Reform, and Reconstructionist. The duties of a rabbi have also grown to meet the demands of the community. Today's rabbis provide spiritual guidance for the members of their synagogue and educational leadership to their community. Many are also involved in interfaith dialogues with other clergy.

The following selection, written by George Robinson, describes the role of the rabbi in each of the branches of Judaism. Although not needed to lead services, a rabbi is necessary as a teacher and decision maker on Jewish law and liturgy. He or she is also the judge of the "correctness" of what is done during a service. George Robinson is a freelance journalist whose work has appeared in the *New York Times, Newsday, Jewish Week*, and the *Detroit Jewish News*. He is also a trustee of Beth Am, a Reform synagogue in New York City.

What is striking about Jewish communal prayer is not merely that it presumes an active dialogue between God and the individual. Christianity asserts similar relationships in individual prayer. What sets Judaism (and Islam) apart is that it believes in *direct* discourse with God without benefit of the intervention of clergy, even in a communal prayer setting. Because Judaism is not a religion based on sacraments like communion, which can only be administered by a priesthood, a Jew doesn't need a rabbi to speak to God, even in a formal religious service. Any ten adult Jews (in traditionally observant practice, adult male Jews) can form a *minyan*, a quorum for prayer, and hold a service in a reasonably appropriate place. In fact, one doesn't even need a *minyan* to hold a service (although there are certain prayers that are communal in nature and are, therefore, omitted from a service at which fewer than ten are present).

Any Jew over the age of thirteen can lead a service, can read from the Torah, can give a sermon. In a women's *tefilah/prayer* group, any girl over twelve can perform these tasks. In Reform, Reconstructionist, and many Conservative congregations, women are counted in a *minyan* and can perform any of the functions allotted in a worship service. The leader in a synagogue service is usually called the *shaliakh tzibbur/messenger of the community;* he (or she in many liberal congregations) functions as reader or cantor, leading worship by repeating aloud certain passages of the liturgy, leading hymns, and so on. The *Shulkhan Arukh*, the medieval digest of Jewish laws that is still the guide for Orthodox Jews, lists six qualities required of a *shaliakh tzibbur:* humility, acceptability to the congregation, knowledge of the rules of prayer and proper pronunciation of Hebrew, an agreeable voice, proper dress, and a beard. The last qualification is waived except for the High Holy Days.

Judaism wasn't always so democratic. When Solomon built the First Temple in Jerusalem, only the priests could perform certain rituals, receiving sacrifices and making them. When that Temple was destroyed in 586 B.C. and the Jewish people were sent into exile in Babylonia, their leaders had to devise new ways of worshipping God. The Temple was rebuilt after their return to Palestine, but with the second and final destruction of the Temple in A.D. 70, it was no longer possible to bring sacrifices and offerings to God as prescribed in Jewish law. With no Temple, there was no place to perform those specific rites. Rituals freed of sacrifices and offerings no longer required a priestly caste. A worship centered on liturgy, on words, rather than on sacraments (as is the case in, say, Christianity), could be led by laymen. (There is one holdover from the days of the Temple in Jerusalem: the schedule of daily services used today—*shakharit/the morning service, minkhah/the afternoon service, ma'ariv/the evening service*—roughly corresponds to the schedule of sacrifices.) . . .

What the Rabbi Does

For the vast majority of modern practicing Jews ever since . . . Judaism is still resolutely nonhierarchical in worship. The distinction between lay leadership and the rabbinate is much narrower in practice and theory than in most Christian denominations.

About the only thing a rabbi can do in front of a congregation that can't be done by an ordinary Jew is sign a marriage license, and that power is not granted by a Jewish body but by the state. A layperson can conduct a funeral or a *kiddushin/sanctification* ceremony for a wedding. (However, even the most progressive congregations will not permit a layperson to be responsible for performing a wedding; there are too many legal questions, issues like witnesses, the rings, etc., to take the risk.)

That being the case, what exactly does a rabbi do in terms of worship? To some extent, the answer to that question depends on the branch of Judaism to which the congregation belongs, the *minhag* [customary religious practice] of the congregation, and even its financial situation.

For example, in a prosperous Conservative synagogue, the congregants may expect services to be led by a polished, highly trained cantor, who will *daven* (Yid-

dish "pray") the entire service, except when there's a
bar mitzvah and the *bar mitzvah* boy or *bat mitzvah* girl
will lead portions of the service. The rabbi may do little more during services than announce page numbers
and deliver a sermon (although the latter is no small
thing!). A less well-to-do congregation may hire a rabbi
who can *daven* well.

In general, in a Reform synagogue the rabbi leads services. For reasons growing out of the evolution of the Reform movement, which had its roots in nineteenth-
century Germany and which in its first century tried to
emulate the style of neighboring Protestant churches,
members of Reform congregations were until recently
less likely to learn to lead services, deferring to the rabbinate and cantorate. The result was a Reform lay population that until the past twenty or so years was less educated in liturgy and worship. In recent years, the Union
of American Hebrew Congregations, the umbrella organization of Reform synagogues in the United States, and
the Central Conference of American Rabbis, the organization representing the Reform rabbinate, have moved
to remedy that problem. In smaller congregations that
lack a full-time rabbi, congregants are now leading services, trained by a rabbinic aide program.

But even with a more educated lay membership, Reform and Conservative rabbis are still an indispensable
part of worship. They are still the most informed in
matters of the laws of traditional liturgy, the most educated about what's going on in the Jewish world litur-
gically, the first to hear when a movement publishes a
new prayerbook. And even in an Orthodox synagogue,
a congregation in which the average layperson is well
qualified to *daven* on his own, it still falls to the rabbi
to decide thorny questions of practice.

Making Sure That What Is Done Is Being Done Right

"The rabbi is necessary as a teacher and as someone to rule on Jewish law, including liturgical questions, but is not needed to lead services," one prominent Reform rabbi told me. "You need someone in the room to make sure that what is done is being done right. There are so many minute details of Jewish law that there has to be someone there who is really learned."

In addition, there are issues of the aesthetics and cultural principles that have to be taken into account in planning worship. "The clergy are still the most educated in planning worship," the rabbi concluded. "Who knows the most about what you have to do to make worship 'work'?"

Regardless of what a rabbi knows or does during worship, he or she cannot intercede with God for the congregation. Ultimately every Jew is responsible for his own conversation with God. And what happens in that dialogue is a matter of great concern in Judaism.

Imagine yourself in conversation with someone you cannot see, someone you have never seen, yet who is omnipresent and omnipotent. Needless to say, left to your own devices, you would probably be rendered speechless or reduced to a handful of mumbled, stammered commonplaces. The rabbis who began the process of setting the liturgy recognized this problem some two thousand years ago, and the establishment of a fixed order of prayers is the way in which they addressed it.

A Jew needn't invent his own prayers to God (although there is space within the liturgy to do so at points in the *Amidah*). She needn't feel that God's response to her worship will be based on how eloquent or poetic her words are. The words are the same at each of the day's services, the same on each Sabbath, on each festival. An observant Jew who prays every day, three times a day, will undoubtedly have memorized large portions of the liturgy. A knowledgeable Jew can walk into a synagogue anywhere in the world and know where she is in the service. But even an occasional synagogue-goer can pick up a *siddur/prayerbook* and follow the service in Hebrew or in translation.

The great medieval Jewish philosopher and legal scholar [Moses] Maimonides [1135–1204], said that the Torah requires that one pray only once a day. He defined prayer to include, at the least, praise, supplication, and thanks, in that order. Prior to the time of Ezra [priest, scribe, and religious reformer] (fifth century B.C.), that is probably what people did. With the Exile after the destruction of the Temple [in 586 B.C.] Hebrew ceased to be the only language spoken by the Jews; as its use became more unnatural for Jews in the Diaspora [the scattering of Jews throughout the world after the Exile], it became necessary to establish fixed prayers.

But the rabbis understood that a fixed liturgy was only a starting point. A Jew who relies on a rote knowledge of the *siddur* to speed through his devotions, who prays without feeling—by rote—is not really praying. "Rabbi Eliezer says, 'When someone makes their prayer *kevah/fixed*, their prayer is not prayer'" (*Mishnah Berakhot 4:4*).

The rabbis of the first century A.D., the great sages of the era in which the liturgy began evolving towards its current form, called prayer "service of the heart," and they understood that the heart must be involved in prayer for prayer to reach to the gates of Heaven. "Prayer," they said, "needs *kavanah*."

Focusing Prayer

What is *kavanah?* Literally translated it means "intention" or "direction." In practice, it refers to the focus and directedness with which one should pray. Referring to the two most important prayers in the Jewish liturgy, Maimonides writes, "The first thing you must do is turn your thoughts away from everything else when you recite the *Shema* or *Amidah*. . . . When you are engaged in the performance of religious duties, have your mind concentrated entirely on what you are doing." (*Guide for the Perplexed*, 3.51). It is written that the pious Jews of old would wait for an hour before reciting the *Amidah*, hoping to develop the appropriate state of mind to speak with God. After all, as Rabbi Eliezer also said in the first century A.D., "When you pray, know before Whom you stand!" Maimonides would add that at the same time one should focus on the content of the words.

Kavanah is undoubtedly responsible for one of the most oft-remarked aspects of Jewish prayer, the swaying to and fro during prayer that one often sees in a synagogue, particularly in an Orthodox congregation. Called *shucklin*, a Yiddish word, this bowing or swaying often grows out of the intensity of feeling experienced by the one praying. The *Zohar*, a key work of Jewish mysticism, says that when a Jew "says one word of Torah, a lamp is kindled and he cannot keep still, but sways to and fro like the flame of a wick." Others attribute this movement to the words of Psalm 35, which says, "All my limbs shall declare, Adonai, who is like You?" It should be noted that swaying during prayer isn't obligatory; in fact there are rabbinical authorities who oppose it, but the general consensus is that if it is an aid to *kavanah* it is acceptable, if not, then not.

Kavanah is also responsible for another aspect of Orthodox worship that many non-Orthodox Jews find disconcerting: everyone prays at his/her own pace, with little of the service repeated in unison. William Helmreich [educator and author] recalls an experience from his childhood in an Orthodox congregation: "To have said each prayer in unison would have inhibited the freedom of expression that enabled us to pray with fervor. Besides, certain words meant more to different people, and at different times, depending on their mood" (*Wake Up, Wake Up, to Do the Work of the Creator* [New York, 1976]).

Many of the enchanting tales of the Hasidic [ultrapious Orthodox] rabbis of the eighteenth and nineteenth centuries illustrate the supreme importance of *kavanah* in worship. One of the best-known concerns the little boy who came with his father to the Yom Kippur service conducted by the Baal Shem Tov, the founder of Hasidism and one of the great figures of eighteenth-century Judaism. The boy had with him a small flute. As the service drew to its dramatic close and shofar was blown to signal the end of this holiest of days, the little boy pulled out the flute and in his excitement he sounded a note of his own, a shrill piercing sound that brought everything to a halt. His father was mortified and infuriated, but the Baal Shem Tov calmed him, saying, "Until that moment there was some doubt if our prayers would ascend to heaven, but at the sound of that flute, the angels held open the gates and all the prayers entered."

The Talmud

by Harry Gersh

Talmud is a Hebrew word meaning "study" or "teach." It is the complex body of discussions on Jewish law (as given in the Torah), ethics, and customs accumulated over a period of seven hundred years. It also contains legends and stories as well as case histories and moral exhortations. Orthodox Jews (the most traditional branch of Judaism) believe that God not only gave the Jews commandments by which to live but also taught Moses how the commandments were to be applied. Moses then taught what he had learned to others. The oral transmission of the law continued until the second century A.D., when it was gathered and written down in a document called the Mishnah. Further commentaries on the Oral Law continued over the centuries and were written down in Jerusalem and in Babylonia, the two main centers of Jewish learning. The additional commentaries on the Oral Law are called the Gemara. Together, the Mishnah and the Gemara make up the Talmud.

The rabbis, or learned teachers, who compiled the Mishnah divided it into six sections or orders. Each order contains several divisions or tractates. Orders expound on agricultural laws, the Sabbath and festivals, questions about marriage and divorce, questions about civil and criminal law, questions dealing with sacrifices, the Temple, dietary laws, and questions about ritual purity and impurity. To study the Talmud is a great privilege and the goal of many observant Jews.

The history of the Talmud is the subject of the following selection. In it author Harry Gersh explains why and how the Talmud was compiled. Gersh also provides background on the learned teachers who carried out the work of compilation. Gersh is a journalist whose articles have appeared in *Commentary*, the *New Republic*, and the *New York Times Magazine*.

If the Bible is the heart of Judaism, of the continuing, persistent Congregation of Israel, the Talmud is the moving, changing bloodstream nourishing every organ and extremity of that corpus. These books, as much as any physical property or intellectual concept, kept the Jews alive as a community, however dispersed, through fifteen hundred years in which all logic dictated their disappearance.

The Talmud

The Talmud is two very distinct books (and book is used here in its very broadest sense): the Mishnah; and the commentary on the Mishnah, the Gemarah. The Mishnah, from the Hebrew *shonah*, to repeat, therefore to study by repetition, is the recorded Oral Law of the Jews in use about the year 200, the period when the Mishnah was finally compiled and edited by Judah haNasi (Judah the Prince). There are two Gemarahs, the Palestinian and the Babylonian, each a record of the comments and discussions of the Mishnah by different schools of rabbis, sages, and scholars. The Mishnah of

Judah haNasi and the Gemarah of the Palestinian scholars make up the *Talmud Yerushalmi*, the Jerusalem (or Palestinian) Talmud. The Mishnah of Judah haNasi and the Gemarah of the Babylonian academies make up the *Talmud Babli*, the Babylonian Talmud.

The deliberations of scholars in Palestine were interrupted many times by persecutions and the unsettled conditions of that country in the centuries after the end of the Second Roman War in 135. Toward the end of the fourth century, times were so desperate that the work was rushed to completion. It was in its final form by 400. The Babylonian scholars lived in a relatively more peaceful and free environment. They could therefore be much more deliberate. The Babylonian Talmud was completed a century after the Palestinian Talmud, about 500. During the period of the compilation of the Talmud and for five hundred years afterward, Babylon was the new Jerusalem, the center of world Jewry. Thus the fuller Babylonian Talmud became the dominant work: when reference is made to *the* Talmud, the Babylonian Talmud is meant; reference to the Palestinian Talmud requires the place-name adjective.

Jewish tradition says that Moses received two Laws on Mt. Sinai: the Torah, or written law, and the Oral Law. . . . The Oral Law, according to the Talmud, was handed down as follows:

> Moses received the [Oral] Law from Sinai and delivered it to Joshua, and Joshua to the elders, and the elders to the Prophets, and the Prophets committed it to the men of the Great Synagogue. . . . Simeon the Just was of the survivors of the Great Synagogue. . . . Antigonus of Socho received it from Simeon the Just. . . . Jose ben Joezer of Zeredah and Jose ben Jochonon of Jerusalem received from them. . . . Joshua ben Perahyah and Nittai the Arbelite received from them. . . .

Judah ben Tabbai and Simeon ben Shetah received from them. . . . Shemaiah and Abtalion received from them. . . . Hillel and Shammai received from them. . . . Jochanon ben Zakkai received [the Law] from Hillel and from Shammai.

The Need for Answers

This genealogy passes quickly over the almost one thousand years between Moses and the men of the Great Synagogue (circa 450–325 B.C.), but it details the later transmission almost generation by generation. This is realistic, because the Oral Law was relatively unimportant during the years of the Judges, the monarchy, the divided kingdoms, and the Babylonian exile—the years of the development of the Torah. As a more or less self-governing nation, the Jews had little need for the collection of adapted customs, interpretations of various decalogues, and common usages that was the Oral Law before 450 B.C. But with their return from Babylon as vassals of a foreign king, and the acceptance by the priestly schools of the realistic probability that the Jews would henceforth always be subject to foreign law, the need for defined religious-secular Judaic law became intense. The need became desperate when the Torah was canonized (400 B.C.) and the Written Law became fixed and unalterable. For despite the Jews' insistence on its divine origin, the Torah, like man-made laws, did not answer all legal questions. It lagged behind the need and the practice in both religious and secular areas.

For example, as soon as the Palestinian Jewish community was well organized, there was need for specific interpretations of the Biblical prohibition of work on the sabbath: "Six days shalt thou labor and do all thy work; but the seventh day is a sabbath onto the Lord thy God. . . ." "Ye shall keep the sabbath, therefore, for it is holy unto you; everyone that profaneth it shall surely be put to death. . . ." But the Mosaic Law identified only three kinds of work prohibited on the sabbath: "Ye shall kindle no fire throughout your habitations upon the sabbath day"; ". . . abide ye every man in his place, let no man go out of his place on the seventh day"; ". . . they found a man gathering sticks on the sabbath day. . . . and [they] stoned him with stones. . . ." Obviously, the work prohibited on the sabbath was not limited to making fire, gathering kindling, and walking outside your "place." And what constitutes "place"?

The Oral Law had begun a redefinition of prohibited work long before the Written Law was closed. [Seventh-century B.C. prophet] Jeremiah reproved people for carrying packages on the sabbath, although this was not specifically barred by the Bible; and [fifth-century B.C. reformer] Nehemiah drove the traders out of Jerusalem on the sabbath, also without Biblical authority. Thus, over centuries the Oral Law widened the meaning of "labor" that "profaneth" the sabbath—always referring to some Biblical authority for the new meanings. The scribes ("men of the book" is a better translation) developed a list of thirty-nine types of prohibited work which they took from the list of jobs itemized in the Bible as necessary to build the Temple. . . .

The men of the Great Synagogue (more properly, Great Assembly) were the first body to assume authority for interpreting the sparse Biblical commandments and developing a law capable of regulating the affairs of an increasingly sophisticated community. Little is known about this body, despite rather frequent mention in the Talmud, but it must have functioned as a combined religious and secular court in post-exilic Palestine. The authority of the Great Assembly was transferred to the Sanhedrin during the Hellenistic period, beginning with the death of Alexander the Great. But the Sanhedrin had more than a single voice. It is assumed by some scholars that the Sanhedrin was a bicameral body, much like the British Parliament before the power of the House of Lords was wiped out. These scholars believe that the upper house of the Sanhedrin (like the Lords) was representative of the priests of the Temple and the ruling class; the lower house (like the Commons) represented the people. Each house became the stronghold of a religious-political party, the upper house of the Sadducees (from Zadok, high priest in the first Temple), the lower house of the Pharisees (separatists). The Sadducees were strict interpreters of the Torah and refused to give any authority to the Oral Law; the Pharisees insisted upon the validity of a developing Oral Law. . . .

The Compilers of the Law

The Sadducees, the royalist nationalistic party, the party of the Temple in Jerusalem, were eliminated as a force in Jewish life when the Romans destroyed their power centers in the Temple and the court and the commonwealth in the year 70. The Pharisees' power, on the other hand, was based on the synagogues; scattered throughout the land, they could withstand the destruction of the religious and governmental centers. Thus the Pharisaic tradition continued, while the Sadducees disappeared. Jochanon ben Zakkai, disciple and successor to the great Hillel and leader of the Pharisees, gathered the surviving scholars of Judah and established an academy in the village of Jabneh. This body assumed the religious and legal authority of the Sanhedrin. (This was the body that canonized the last section of the Bible in the year 90). During the sixty years of peace—comparative peace—from 70 to 130, the Academy at Jabneh adapted Jewish law to the new conditions of Jewish life, the life of a dispersed nation without king or title to any land. At Jabneh the sages began compiling and ordering the great body of civil and religious and ethical legislation that existed outside the Bible, existed only in the trained memories of the scholars.

Early in the second century, the leading scholar among the compilers of the Oral Law was Rabbi Akiba ben Joseph, one of the great romantic figures of Jewish history and the architect of the Mishnah. According to Jewish tradition, Akiba was an unlettered workman until he was forty years old; then he turned to a life of scholarship and became the greatest scholar and teacher of his generation. He was martyred by the Romans during the Bar Kochba rebellion, the Second Roman War, for refusing to heed their order prohibiting the teaching of the Torah.

Rabbi Akiba had two scholarly passions: to find a Biblical source for every law and judgment and opinion in the developing Oral Law, and to organize the Oral Law so that it would be readily available and readily applicable to every condition. The first pursuit led Rabbi Akiba into some rather tenuous interpretations; the second led to the Mishnah of Rabbi Akiba, whose structure and organization was the basis of the Talmud.

With the complete destruction of the Palestinian community after the defeat of Bar Kochba and the persecutions under Emperor Hadrian, the Jewish academies were closed, and the disciples and sages were dispersed. But the need for maintaining and transmitting the Oral Law was intensified. This task was carried forward by Akiba's greatest disciple, Rabbi Meir. Building on Rabbi Akiba's framework, his student erected the Mishnah of Rabbi Meir.

The real authorities among the Jews, even during the last years of the Hasmonean kings, were the chief scholars of the community, the heads of the Sanhedrin before the year 70, and the hereditary patriarchs after the destruction of the Temple. The two groups of rulers were really one, since the patriarchs were the descendants of Hillel, head of the Sanhedrin from 30 B.C. to the year 10. (The only nonmember of the House of Hillel to head the ruling council—from 70 to 90—was Jochanon ben Zakkai.)

Judah haNasi, called simply Rabbi, held the patriarchate from 165 to 219. He was born, according to tradition, on the day that Rabbi Akiba was martyred. Legend endows Rabbi with every positive attribute: he was very wise, very rich, and personally beautiful; he had the friendship of Roman emperors, very deserving children, and a long life. Although the Mishnah doesn't actually say that Rabbi was the final editor and redactor of the Mishnah, the Talmud (both Jerusalem and Babylonian) accepts the fact without question.

Rabbi, himself a great scholar, gathered a remarkable school of sages and with them put together the final Mishnah. Through the authority of his scholarship and of his status in the world Jewish community, Rabbi's Mishnah became the accepted standard of Jewish law. . . .

Constructing the Gemarah

Cyrus of Babylon had released the Captivity and permitted the exiled Jews to return to Palestine toward the end of the sixth century B.C. But, much like the case of twentieth-century Israel, only a minority of Jews returned to the Holy Land. The majority remained in Babylonia; considering the later histories of the two communities, particularly during the three centuries ending with the Second Roman (or Jewish) War in 135, the choice was reasonable. The Persian kings were, in the main, far more tolerant of their Jewish subjects than the successive overlords and rulers of Palestine. And unlike the dispersed congregations of Jews to the West, the Babylonian Jews held tightly to the ties with Palestine. They accepted the authority of the Temple, of the Palestinian academies, and of the Palestinian patriarchs. Although the Babylonian Jews had active scholarly academies of their own, they sent their brightest pupils to be trained in the Jerusalem centers of learning.

Among the students in Jerusalem during the final redaction of the Mishnah was Abba Areka, son of a distinguished Babylonian family and foremost student-disciple of Judah haNasi. Abba Areka, called Rab, returned to his native country and established an academy at Sura, on the Euphrates River. This academy became one of the great centers of Jewish learning—and remained so for more than seven hundred years.

Another Babylonian student at the Jerusalem academy was Samuel, called Mar [Aramaic for "Lord"], who returned to Babylonia to become head of the academy at Nehardea. Like so many Jewish scholars before the modern period, Mar Samuel was renowned not only for his scholarship in Judaic studies but also for other scholarly pursuits; he was a great astronomer and a much sought-after physician. At their respective academies, Abba Areka and Mar Samuel began the process that was to result in the Gemarah.

In 259, the city of Nehardea was destroyed during a Roman-Persian war. The Nehardea Academy was re-established in the city of Pumbeditha—and it, too, lasted more than seven hundred years. In those centuries, beginning with Mar Samuel and Abba Areka, generation after generation of scholars—the *amoraim*—participated in the study of the Mishnah and in the accumulation of comment, explanatory material, and illustrative stories that was to form the Gemarah.

Using the Mishnah as a text, the scholars at the academies analyzed the Oral Law and its basis in the Written Law—line by line. The analysis—in fact, the dissection—was aimed at uncovering the meaning behind the meaning, the source behind the source. Most of the material offered to make or support an argument was relevant, but as with most discussions of points of law in any country and period, some of the comments and explanations wandered far afield. And in wandering so far afield, the commentaries encompassed the entire body of Jewish knowledge of the time. Thus, in the Gemarah, on the Mishnaic section dealing with the division of property, there is discussion of the line: "Sacred writings, however, may not be divided. . . ." In the course of this discussion, there is an analysis of the meaning and relevance of Scripture. This seeming side issue takes twenty pages of the Talmud. . . .

As with the Mishnah before Rabbi Akiba gave it a structure, the Gemarah grew without limit or form for two centuries. In 375, Rab Ashi became head of the academy at Sura and began the process of compilation and order. During more than a half-century of leadership of the academy (375–427), Rab Ashi assembled the great commentary on the Mishnah. He not only performed for the Gemarah the counterpart of Rabbi Judah haNasi's work on the Mishnah; he was also very much like Rabbi, as rich in worldly goods and in spiritual and scholarly attainments. Unlike Judah haNasi, Rab Ashi did not close his book; that took another seventy years or so, but the form of the Talmud was fixed by Ashi.

Throughout this period, from the closing of the Mishnah until about 400, the Palestinian Talmud and the Babylonian Talmud developed independently—but cooperatively. Scholars moved regularly back and forth between the Babylonian academies and the Palestinian academies at Caesarea, Sepphoris, and Tiberias, transmitting the discussions and opinions. Rab Ashi's Gemarah, therefore, includes much material that had been developed in Palestine.

For a time after Ashi's death, the Persians were infected with missionary zeal and tried to suppress the Jews, hoping to convert them to Zoroastrianism. The students were scattered and teaching was forbidden. It was time to close the Babylonian Talmud. When the persecutions abated, the discussions were rounded out, legal points were sharpened, and additional homiletic material was added. The final touches were made by the master of the Sura Academy known as Rabbina II. On his death in 499, the Babylonian Talmud was closed.

The Printed Talmud

The Talmud is unique not only in content but also in form and pagination. A page of the Talmud beginning a section has in the center the *mishnah* under discussion; around it is written the *gemarah* interpreting and discussing the *mishnah;* in the margins are comments by noted sages. . . .

The Mishnah was first printed in 1492 in Naples by

the Soncino Press. The first printed Talmud was produced by Daniel Bomberg in Venice, 1520. Every printed version of the Talmud since that day has exactly the same paging. Whether a Talmud was printed in Amsterdam, Vilna, Berlin, or New York, in the seventeenth or eighteenth or twentieth centuries, each page begins with the same word and ends with the same word. Thus, a reference to page 60b of the tractate Gittin is the same in any edition printed by any press at any time.

Moses Mendelssohn: A Famous Thinker

by Shira Schoenberg

Jews were forced from their ancient homeland following the destruction by the Romans of the Temple in
Jerusalem in A.D. 70. With this event Palestinian Jews
dispersed throughout the eastern Mediterranean region
and beyond. As a result of this dispersion, or diaspora,
Jewish scholars came in greater contact with non-Jews,
non-Jewish culture, and different schools of philosophy. Philo Judaeus (20 B.C. to A.D. 50), a Jew from the
Egyptian city of Alexandria, wrote in Greek and showed
the influences of the Greek philosopher Plato in his
writings about the ideal world. Moses Maimonides
(1135 to 1204), a Spanish-born Jew trained in medicine,
tried to reconcile the teachings of the Greek philosopher Aristotle and the Torah, or Jewish Law. In the modern era, Moses Mendelssohn (1729–1786) remained an
observant Jew while exploring the philosophy of rationalism. Mendelssohn was also an activist within German society. He spoke out for the rights of German
Jews and also helped modernize German Jewish culture by urging Jews to pursue secular educations. One
of his accomplishments was the translation of the
Bible into High German, thereby making it accessible
to non-Jewish Germans. Mendelssohn is regarded as the

father of the Jewish Enlightenment, or *Haskalah*. German Jewish thinkers of the Enlightenment discussed ways of remaining true to the tenets of Judaism while making Judaism understandable in a rational way. The Jewish Enlightenment gave birth to the rise of Reform Judaism, one of the branches of contemporary Judaism.

Moses Mendelssohn is profiled in the following brief biography by Shira Schoenberg, a freelance writer and educator. It is taken from the Jewish Virtual Library Web site at www.jewishvirtuallibrary.org.

Moses Mendelssohn was the first Jew to bring secular culture to those living an Orthodox [traditional] Jewish life. He valued reason and felt that anyone could arrive logically at religious truths. He argued that what makes Judaism unique is its divine revelation of a code of law. He wrote many philosophical treatises and is considered the father of the Jewish Enlightenment.

Moses Mendelssohn was born in Dessau, a city in the state of Anhalt-Dessan in Germany, on September 6, 1729. As a child, he suffered from a disease that left him with a curvature of the spine. He was the son of a Torah [Jewish law] scribe, and his family was poor but learned. He began a traditional Jewish education under David Fraenkel, the rabbi of Dessau. When Fraenkel became rabbi of Berlin, the 14-year-old Mendelssohn followed him and studied in Fraenkel's yeshiva [school where Jewish religious texts are studied] in Berlin. He soon became a promising scholar of Talmud [body of Jewish law and lore] and Rabbinics. He is a relative of Samson Raphael Hirsch [a nineteenth-century German rabbi known as the Father of Neo-Orthodoxy]. He received free meals from neighborhood families and took on odd tutoring jobs.

In addition to learning German and Hebrew in Berlin, Mendelssohn also studied some French, Italian, English, Latin and Greek. He took up other secular [non-religious] subjects, in which he excelled, including mathematics, logic and philosophy. In the mid-1750s, he developed friendships with the philosopher Immanuel Kant [who lived from 1724–1804] and also with Gotthold Lessing, a dramatist, literary critic and advocate of enlightened toleration in Germany. With Lessing's encouragement, Mendelssohn began to publish philosophical essays in German.

In 1750, Mendelssohn began to serve as a teacher in the house of Isaac Bernhard, the owner of a silk factory. That same year, Frederick the Great [king of Prussia who lived from 1712–1786] gave him the status of "Jew under extraordinary protection." In 1763, the Prussian Academy of Sciences awarded him a prize for his treatise on "evidence in the metaphysical sciences." Four years later, he became the bookkeeper of Bernhard's firm and eventually a partner. Throughout his life, he worked as a merchant while continuing to write. In 1779, Lessing wrote the play *Nathan the Wise* in which a Jewish hero, modeled after Mendelssohn, appears as a spokesman for brotherhood and love of humanity.

His Ideas on Religion

Mendelssohn modeled his philosophy after that of Christian Wolff (a prominent philosopher of the Enlightenment) and Gottfried Leibnitz (a European rationalist). He wrote some general philosophical works, including many dealing with the theory of art, but his most well known writings deal with Judaism. Mendelssohn conceived of God as a perfect Being and had faith in God's wisdom, righteousness, mercy and goodness. He argued that, "the world results from a creative act through which the divine will seeks to realize the highest good." He accepted the existence of miracles and revelation as long as belief in God did not depend on them. He also believed that revelation could not contradict reason. Like the deists [who believe in God as the Creator of the Universe but do not follow a "revealed" religion], he claimed that reason could discover the reality of God, divine providence and immortality of the soul. He was the first to speak out against the use of excommunication as a religious threat.

At the height of his career, in 1769, Mendelssohn was publicly challenged by a Christian apologist [defender], a Zurich pastor named John Lavater, to defend the superiority of Judaism over Christianity. From then on, he was involved in defending Judaism in print. In 1783, he published *Jerusalem, or On Religious Power and Judaism.* This study posited that no religious institution should use coercion and emphasized that Judaism does not coerce the mind through dogma [formal doctrine]. He argued that through reason all people could discover religious philosophical truths, but what made Judaism unique was its divinely revealed code of legal, ritual and moral law. He said that Jews must live in civil society but only in a way that their right to observe religious laws is granted. He recognized the necessity of multiple religions and respected each one.

Mendelssohn wanted to take the Jews out of a ghetto [segregated community] lifestyle and into secular society. He translated the Bible into German, although it was written in Hebrew letters, with a Hebrew commentary called the *Biur.* He campaigned for emancipation [freedom from bondage] and instructed Jews to form bonds with the gentile [non-Jewish] governments. He tried to improve the relationship between Jews and Christians as he argued for tolerance and humanity. He became the symbol of the Jewish Enlightenment, the *Haskalah.*

Mendelssohn's own descendants, the most famous being the composer Felix Mendelssohn, left Judaism for Christianity.

Sources

Cohn-Sherbok, Dan. *Fifty Key Jewish Thinkers.* New York: Routledge, 1997.

Dimont, Max. *Jews, God and History.* New York: Simon & Schuster, 1962.

Kleinman, Shanon. "Who Was Moses Mendelssohn?" *Hamevaser.*

Kung, Hans. *Judaism.* New York: Crossroad, 1992.

Seltzer, Robert. *Jewish People, Jewish Thought.* New York: Macmillan Publishing Co., 1980.

I and Thou

by Martin Buber

Austrian-born Martin Buber (1878–1965) was one of the most important Jewish philosophers of the twentieth century. His philosophy of dialogue is described in *I and Thou*, published in 1923. In this work Buber sets forth his social and religious philosophy by noting the differences in types of relationships. In the "I-Thou" relationship humans relate to the world with openness, directness, and a sense of mutual sympathy. There is a real, interpersonal dialogue between individuals in this kind of relationship because the parties regard each other as having unique value. The other type of relationship, the "I-It," lacks these qualities because it is essentially a monologue in which each party views the other as having only utilitarian value. The highest expression of the "I-Thou" relationship is the bond forged between individuals and God, referred to as the "Eternal Thou" by Buber. The philosophy of Martin Buber heavily influenced philosophers of other faiths, such as Karl Barth, Paul Tillich, and Reinhold Niebuhr. Buber's ideas can be seen at work in the theory of interpersonal communications.

Buber was also a translator of the Bible, a journalist, an educator, an author (*Between Man and Man, Pointing the Way*), and a Zionist (one who supported the founding of a national homeland for the Jews). When the

Martin Buber, *I and Thou*. New York: Charles Scribner's Sons, 1958.

155

Nazis seized power in Germany in 1933 and began a systematic persecution of the Jews, Buber resigned his post as professor of religion at the University of Frankfurt but continued to teach Judaism until it became impossible for him to do so. In 1938 he moved to Palestine (now Israel) where he lived, taught, and advocated dialogue between Jews and Christians and between Arabs and Jews. Buber stated that "all real living is meeting." Up until his death he remained totally alive and open to the moment, meeting others—human to human—in dialogue.

The following excerpt is from *I and Thou*.

———————————

To man the world is twofold, in accordance with his twofold attitude.

He perceives what exists round about him—simply things, and beings as things; and what happens round about him—simply events, and actions as events; things consisting of qualities, events of moments; things entered in the graph of place, events in that of time; things and events bounded by other things and events, measured by them, comparable with them: he perceives an ordered and detached world. It is to some extent a reliable world, having density and duration. Its organisation can be surveyed and brought out again and again; gone over with closed eyes, and verified with open eyes. It is always there, next to your skin, if you look on it that way, cowering in your soul, if you prefer it so. It is your object, remains it as long as you wish, and remains a total stranger, within you and without. You perceive it, take it to yourself as the "truth," and it lets itself be taken; but it does not give itself to you. Only concerning it may you make yourself "understood" with others; it is ready, though attached to everyone in a different way, to be an object common to you all. But you cannot meet others in it. You cannot hold on to life without it, its reliability sustains you; but should you die in it, your grave would be in nothingness.

Or on the other hand, man meets what exists and becomes as what is over against him, always simply a *single* being and each thing simply as being. What exists is opened to him in happenings, and what happens affects him as what is. Nothing is present for him except this one being, but it implicates the whole world. Measure and comparison have disappeared; it lies with yourself how much of the immeasurable becomes reality for you. These meetings are not organised to make the world, but each is a sign of the world-order. They are not linked up with one another, but each assures you of your solidarity with the world. The world which appears to you in this way is unreliable, for it takes on a continually new appearance; you cannot hold it to its word. It has no density, for everything in it penetrates everything else; no duration, for it comes even when it is not summoned, and vanishes even when it is tightly held. It cannot be surveyed, and if you wish to make it capable of survey you lose it. It comes, and comes to bring *you* out; if it does not reach you, meet you, then it vanishes; but it comes back in another form. It is not outside you, it stirs in the depth of you; if you say "Soul of my soul" you have not said too much. But guard against wishing to remove it into your soul—for then you annihilate it. It is your present; only while you have it do you have the present. You can make it into an object for yourself, to experience and to use; you must continually do this—and as you do it you have no more present. Between you and it there is mutual giving: you say *Thou* to it and give yourself to it, it says *Thou* to you and gives itself to you. You cannot make yourself understood with others concerning it, you are alone with it. But it teaches you to meet others, and to hold your ground when you meet them. Through the graciousness of its comings and the solemn sadness of its goings it leads you away to the *Thou* in which the parallel lines of relations meet. It does not help to sustain you in life, it only helps you to glimpse eternity.

CHAPTER 5

Challenges Facing Jews Today

Marriage Between Jews and Non-Jews

by Samuel G. Freedman

Interfaith marriage, a marriage between two people of different religious backgrounds, is an issue of much concern to Jews. Because Jewish culture is identified so strongly with the religion of Judaism many Jews see interfaith marriage as a threat to their cultural identity. The strongest opponents of interfaith marriage argue that it could lead to the disappearance of the Jewish people. The issue of intermarriage has divided American Jews into several camps: secularists, who view Judaism as their heritage and who do not consider religion important when choosing a wife or husband; liberal branches of Judaism (Reform and Conservative), which acknowledge the legality of interfaith marriage; and traditionalists (Orthodox), who follow the Bible's prohibition against intermarriage unless the non-Jewish partner converts to Judaism.

Any interfaith marriage has implications for the children of such a union. Who are they? According to traditional Jewish law (halacha), a child's religion follows that of the mother. Reform Judaism recognizes a child as Jewish regardless of which parent is Jewish as long as the child has received a Jewish education and identifies with the Jewish community. In the following selection, author Samuel G. Freedman presents the topic of "Who is a Jew?" from both the American Jewish and Israeli Jewish perspectives.

Samuel G. Freedman is a professor of journalism at Columbia University's Graduate School of Journalism. His other books include *The Inheritance: How Three Families and America Moved from Roosevelt to Reagan and Beyond, Upon This Rock,* and *Small Victories.*

The more that secular Judaism declined as a force in American Jewish life, the more it abdicated the task of defining Jewish identity to religious authorities. And once the debate became a religious debate, it was conducted on Orthodox Jewry's ground. The Reform and Conservative movements might hold the allegiance of the vast majority of affiliated American Jews, but the Orthodox by their refusal to compromise *halakhah* [religious law] with modernism seemed to embody authenticity, and they were not timid about dictating the terms of it to every other branch. With their common foe, secularism, now spent, the Jewish denominations turned against one another.

"Judaism the religion had existed in tandem with this other thing we might call Jewishness as ethnicity, Jewishness as peoplehood," says the historian Hasia Diner. "If you asked someone in 1910 what made them Jewish, it might be going to the Yiddish theater, belonging to a Jewish union. They didn't sit around asking what it meant to be Jewish. They lived in a Jewish world. But when that life disappeared or evolved into nostalgia, the religious core that was always there was revealed. And as it was revealed, the religious struggle was exposed."

Nowhere was that struggle more divisive than in the so-called "Who is a Jew?" issue. The phrase actually covered several related elements of Jewish status—intermarriage, conversion, the legitimacy of the non-Orthodox rabbinate. While none of these conflicts was unprecedented in Jewish history, rarely if ever had they imperiled [posed a danger to] communal unity. Jewish tradition had long held that any prospective convert be turned away three times from the synagogue door. *Halakhah* rejected intermarriage so completely that when such unions failed, the Jewish spouse was not even required to obtain the rabbinical divorce decree known as a *get*. Only in modern America did disputes over status reach a critical apogee [high point]. For when it came to whom a Jew loved and married and had children with, the interest of America in a common national culture and the interest of Judaism in tribal continuity were diametrically opposed.

"Embracing the American Way"

During the Jewish emancipation in Europe, the poet Heinrich Heine had described baptism as "an entrance ticket" to the larger society, but even those like him who chose it remained ineffably alien to their host country. In the United States, a nation without a state religion, a pioneer land that allowed every citizen to reinvent himself, the ultimate act of belonging took place at the wedding altar. When Jews intermarry, as the historian Jack Wertheimer has written, "they are embracing the American way."

During the heyday of secular Judaism, the rate of intermarriage between Jews and gentiles [non-Jews] barely exceeded that between whites and blacks. From the early twenties through the late fifties, the share of such marriages crept up only from 1.7 to 6.6 percent; such shame attached to "marrying out" that Jewish parents often observed the mourning ritual of shiva for a child who did so. Then, with the opening of suburbia and private colleges to Jews and the retrenchment of anti-Semitism, the percentage of interfaith marriages nearly doubled in the early sixties and almost tripled during the late sixties and early seventies, reaching about one-third. The kind of Jewish-gentile union that had qualified as a novelty early in the century with the hit play *Abie's Irish Rose* looked more like documentary realism in the television sitcom "Bridget Loves Bernie."

The alarms about Jewish survival rang at several junctures. In 1964, the mass-circulation magazine *Look* published a major article on "The Vanishing American Jew," which gravely discussed the intermarriage rate. In the early seventies, the first National Jewish Population survey showed the intermarriage number at its highest level yet, 31 percent. Twenty years later, the next such survey put the figure at 52 percent. Strictly speaking, a Jew marrying another Jew was now the exception rather than the rule in America. Even those scholars and journalists who disputed the 1990 survey's accuracy placed the intermarriage rate at around 40 percent.

And marriage connoted children, most of whom were adrift from Jewish identity. Only 28 percent of intermarried couples were raising their children solely as Jews; only 13 percent of intermarried couples were affiliated with any branch of Judaism. One in six households that called itself Jewish in the 1990 survey had no member who was a Jew by birth or formal conversion; for those families evidently Jewish identity was not something to be earned or inherited but merely declared. Some 664,000 children under eighteen were not uniformly recognized as Jewish.

One hopeful line of reasoning saw in conversion the solution to Jewish continuity. The demographer Egon Mayer found that parents in a "conversionary" marriage were far more likely than those in a mixed marriage to provide their children with Jewish education and observance. Leaders of Reform Jewry in the late seventies began promoting the search for converts as a fulfillment of God's injunction that Jews be "a light unto nations." In an evolving corpus of memoirs—Paul Cowan's *An Orphan in History*, Stephen Dubner's *Turbulent Souls*, and Gabrielle Glaser's *Strangers to the Tribe*—writers who had been reared as gentiles rediscovered their Jewish heritage.

At the same time, however, conversion only deepened the schisms [divisions] over Jewish identity. Each branch of Judaism maintained separate standards for conversion and no branch accepted the converts of a less observant branch. In the decades of mass immigration, when Orthodoxy dominated American Judaism, these disparities mattered little. In the postwar suburban era, though, the Reform and Conservative movements boomed, representing eighty percent of all affiliated American Jews by 1990, and conducting an even greater share of all conversions. The Reform and Reconstructionist branches both departed from the traditional standard of matrilineal descent [descent from the mother]. Under their new definition, it didn't matter which of a child's parents was Jewish as long as the child was being brought up exclusively as a Jew. And more than one-third of Reform rabbis by the late nineties were performing interfaith weddings.

The distress in Orthodox circles was profound. "A

Holocaust of our own making," Sol Roth, a philosophy professor at Yeshiva University, termed intermarriage in 1980. Over time, his phrase was shortened and coarsened to "Silent Holocaust," and that term enjoyed widespread use among both Modern Orthodox and *haredim* [ultra-Orthodox]. Whether or not Jewish intermarriage constituted autogenocide [self-annihilation] it contributed, along with low birth rates and a sharp decline in Jewish immigration to the shrinking of American Jewry. While the raw number of American Jews rose slightly from decade to decade after World War II, their proportion of the American population fell from 3.6 percent in 1940 to 2.3 percent in 1990. And even if all 180,000 converts were instantly, magically accepted by Orthodox authorities, these self-proclaimed "Jews by choice" comprised less than 5 percent of the American Jewish population, hardly a foundation for continuity.

The love story of Jews and gentiles in America, though, supplied only part of the combustibility of the "Who is a Jew?" issue. The rest resulted from the tangle of religion, politics, and law in Israel. In both real and symbolic ways, American Jews looked to Israel for their cues, and Israel exacerbated American frictions more often than it ameliorated them. Ironically, as the Israeli legal scholar Asher Maoz has pointed out, much of the discord arose from the very law meant to enshrine Jewish unity.

Decisions Made in Israel

The Israeli parliament, the Knesset, unanimously adopted the Law of Return in 1950. While guaranteeing all Jews the right to immigrate to Israel and receive immediate citizenship there, it deliberately avoided defining Jewish identity by any religious measure. Secularists dominated both of Israel's major political parties, the rightist Herut as much as the leftist Mapam, and for both, the law fulfilled the Zionist promise of homeland and refuge from a gentile world that had just finished demonstrating its hatred in the Holocaust [the Nazi destruction of European Jews during World War II].

Yet conflicts underlay the law, too, because of the Zionist tradition of conflating [joining together] religious authority and civil affairs. Decades before Israel achieved statehood, Theodor Herzl drew the religious Mizrachi movement into the Zionist cause by promising autonomy to Orthodox rabbis in a Jewish state. Under both Ottoman [Turkish] and British rule in Palestine, for that matter, Jewish religious leaders had enjoyed similar power. It was no coincidence that Israel, once established, chose a prayer shawl as its flag and the seven-armed candelabra of the Second Temple as its symbol. Arch-secularist though he was, David Ben-Gurion, the founding prime minister, granted rabbinical courts sole jurisdiction over marriage and burial, provided state support for religious schools, and permitted military exemptions for yeshiva [rabbinical] students. In part, Ben-Gurion was practicing smart coalition politics; in part, he was acting on the belief that Orthodoxy would soon wither away.

It did not, of course, and under the pressure of intermarriage and conversion in the Diaspora [Jewish community outside Israel], the inherent contradictions of the Israeli system exploded. A series of cases forced the Israeli Supreme Court to begin answering the question that the Law of Return had studiously avoided: Who exactly is a Jew? In the so-called Brother Daniel case of 1962, the court sided against a Carmelite monk who had been born Jewish and imbued with Zionism before converting to Catholicism in a concentration camp. As a professed Christian, the court decided, Brother Daniel could not simultaneously claim still to be an ethnic Jew. The next major case, however, involved a gentile woman from Scotland who had married an Israeli man and was raising their children in Israel. Rebuffed by the Israeli Ministry of the Interior when they tried to register the children as Jewish, Ruth and Benjamin Shalit in 1970 won a reversal from the nation's Supreme Court.

The Knesset responded with an awkward, troublesome compromise, amending the Law of Return to be simultaneously more lenient and more strict. For purposes of immigration, anyone with a Jewish grandparent would receive immediate citizenship; but for purposes of national registration, Jewish identity was defined by matrilineal descent or "legitimate" conversion. To add to the confusion, the amendment avoided specifying the criteria for a legitimate conversion. No longer was the question of status simply, "Who is a Jew?" Now it was also "Who is a convert?" and "Who is a rabbi?" In Israel, a homogeneous country with an overwhelmingly Orthodox rabbinate, these fine points of debate mattered little. In America, with its boom in both intermarriage and Reform and Conservative affiliation, they could hardly have mattered more.

Initially at least, American interests prevailed. After the Interior Ministry refused to register as Jewish an immigrant named Susan Miller, who had converted under Reform auspices in Colorado, the Israeli Supreme Court in 1986 ordered the recognition of conversions conducted "in any Jewish community abroad." In a later case, the high court criticized the Interior Ministry for denying Jewish recognition to a Brazilian immigrant who had been converted by Reform authorities in Israel, though it did not order a reversal.

But what looked like the triumph of American-style pluralism instead provoked an unprecedented split between American Jewry and the Jewish state, as well as rifts between American Jewish branches. In the late eighties, the ultra-Orthodox bloc in the Knesset held the balance of power between Labor and Likud [political parties]. Courting the religious parties' support for his hawkish stance on the peace process, Prime Minister Yitzhak Shamir promised in May 1987 to introduce an amendment to the Law of Return requiring the Chief Rabbinate to approve all conversions. This meant essentially that only Orthodox conversions would pass muster. In both July 1987 and June 1988, the Knesset debated and defeated the measure. In November 1988, just after the Orthodox bloc had added several seats in the most recent Knesset elections, rumors swirled that Shamir would cut a political deal to ensure passage of the conversion amendment.

The Reaction in America

Much of American Jewry reacted with fury and panic. "Israel is the battlefield, but the war is in America," said Ismar Schorsch, the chancellor of the Jewish Theological Seminary, a Conservative institution. As the United Jewish Appeal [UJA] dispatched an elite delegation to lobby Shamir against the conversion bill, the UJA's chairman, Martin Stein, declared, "This issue goes right to the kishke [Yiddish word for *gut*]." The American Jewish Congress branded the legislation "a betrayal of Israel's partnership with Diaspora Jewry." Yet American Jews were themselves divided. The Lubavitcher Hasidim [an ultra-Orthodox sect] had poured millions of dollars from their Brooklyn headquarters into support for the amendment. In a full-page advertisement in the *New York Times*, an array of American Orthodox groups from the *haredi* Agudath Israel of America to the centrist Rabbinical Council of America, blamed the Reform and Conservative movements for breaking with "a clear definition of Jewish identity that was universally accepted among all Jews for thousands of years." Citing the intermarriage rate in America, the ad went on, "The floodgate of disintegration and demise are beating down our very doors.

The crisis over conversion law subsided when Shamir chose to form a national unity government with Labor, depriving the religious parties of their leverage. But the underlying conflict never went away, any more than intermarriage in America ceased or the Reform and Conservative movements disappeared. In 1997, in fact, the "Who is a Jew?" issue returned with a vengeance. The ultra-Orthodox parties, now part of Benjamin Netanyahu's ruling coalition, introduced a bill to give the Chief Rabbinate control over conversion. Like Shamir before him, Netanyahu was torn between his religious constituency and an inflamed American Jewry; unlike Shamir, he also faced the task of integrating into Israel two hundred thousand Russian immigrants who were not Jewish according to *halakhah*. Israel now had a reason of its own for reconsidering conversion standards.

Netanyahu appointed a commission led by a cabinet minister, Yaakov Ne'eman, to seek a compromise. Its seven members included one apiece from the Reform and Conservative movements—just enough for those branches to denounce their seats as tokenism and for the ultra-Orthodox to object to the mere presence of other branches. Twice, first in the summer and then in the fall of 1997, the commission missed its deadline for delivering its recommendations. When word leaked in October that the Ne'eman Commission would propose a conversion institute operated jointly by all three denominations, the ultra-Orthodox Shas party threatened to bolt from Netanyahu's coalition, toppling his government.

Finally, in January 1998, the commission unveiled its plan. Indeed, it called for rabbis from all three major branches to jointly educate the conversion candidates in a powerful symbol of collaboration and mutual respect. The task of officiating at the actual conversion ceremonies, however, would rest with the Chief Rabbinate, and the Chief Rabbinate made it instantly clear it had no intention of doing so. "There can be no cooperation" with those "who try to shake the foundation of the Jewish religion," the rabbinate declared in a formal resolution. The Reform and Conservative movements, it continued, have "brought about disastrous results of assimilation among Diaspora Jewry." In slightly more refined language, then, the Chief Rabbinate was decrying the Silent Holocaust.

The disparagement of non-Orthodox Judaism and the continuing controversy over Jewish identity weighed far more heavily on America than on Israel. When the news magazine *Jerusalem Report* asked its readers in 1998 to name Israel's most important issue, only 7 percent pointed to conversion standards. Even Tommy Lapid, a politician and commentator known for his flagrant Orthodox-bashing, accused the Reform and Conservative movements of meddling in Israeli affairs. The Ne'eman Commission's institute opened in early 1999 with a mere thirty-seven candidates, all Russian immigrants.

Women and Judaism: A Reform Rabbi Speaks

by Malka Drucker

Reform Judaism, also called Liberal and Progressive Judaism, is one of three main denominations of contemporary Judaism. The other two denominations are Orthodox, the most traditional form of Judaism, and Conservative Judaism, a middle-ground approach that strives to preserve the traditions of Orthodox Judaism while modifying Jewish laws to meet the needs of the present day. Conservative Judaism is the largest branch of Judaism in the United States. A fourth and much smaller branch, Reconstructionism, emphasizes Judaism as an evolving religious civilization open to change.

The Jewish Enlightenment (*Haskalah* in Hebrew) of the eighteenth century saw great changes in how Judaism was practiced. Reformers advocated saying prayers and delivering sermons in the everyday language of the people instead of in Hebrew, the language of the Bible. This movement—aimed at modernizing Judaism—led to the rise of Reform Judaism. Reform rabbis presented Judaism as an evolving set of beliefs instead of an unchanging body of rules and regulations. Reform Judaism was widely adopted in the United States in the 1800s and, in a statement of beliefs issued in Pittsburgh in 1885, described itself as "a progressive religion, ever striving to be in accord with the postulates of reason." Worship services were held once a week rather than every day, and the rabbi's sermon gained greater importance than the actual prayer service. Today the Reform movement is the most inclusive branch of Judaism, ordaining women as rabbis and holding outreach programs for gays and lesbians and non-Jewish spouses in interfaith marriages.

In the following article taken from her Web site, Malka Drucker of HaMakom Congregation in Santa Fe, New Mexico, explains why she is a Reform rabbi. Rabbi Drucker is the author of several books, including a biography of Mexican artist Frida Kahlo, *The Family Treasury of Jewish Holidays*, and *White Fire: A Portrait of Women Spiritual Leaders in America.*

Conceived by the radical thought of Moses Mendelssohn [Jewish philosopher who lived from 1729 to 1786] striving to bring an ancient tradition into the new world of the Enlightenment, and birthed in America in the mid-nineteenth century by the pragmatic Isaac Mayer Wise and the brilliant intellectual, David Einhorn, Reform Judaism is my first religion. At five years old, I experienced Sinai at Central Synagogue in Rockville Centre. The larger-than-life man in a black robe who handed me my consecration Torah [the first five books of the Bible] was none other than Rabbi Roland Gittelsohn.

My parents believed that he spoke the truth. They had rejected the medieval, mysterious, and seemingly meaningless Judaism of their grandparents, and in their search for a way to be Jewish that didn't offend their aesthetics or their ethics, they had found a teacher in the then young visionary who would be a primary force in post-war American Reform Judaism. My parents' passion for a moral, non-ritualistic Judaism was so strong that I assumed that *kashrut* [Jewish dietary laws] had ended when the Temple [site of Jewish worship in Jerusalem] was destroyed in A.D. 70.

When my parents became Reform Jews, they fit into a generation who found traditional Judaism irrelevant, embarrassing, and oppressive. Reform Judaism gave them a Judaism of which they could be proud. Here was a tradition that made sense, and guided not by law but by history. Of all denominations, Reform Judaism may be the one that has most kept Judaism alive. Michael Meyer writes, "There is no decisive event or individual by which one can mark the onset of the Reform movement. Its beginnings lie in the gradual rise of sentiment favoring proposals for doctrinal or practical religious reform prompted by increasing exposure to the world outside the ghetto whose values and demands, gradually internalized and accepted, are perceived to conflict with the inherited tradition." Since its modest beginnings, Reform Judaism has opened its doors wide enough to include many like my parents. "Though the agency of *Wissenschaft des Judentums* [scientific study of Judaism]," David Ellenson writes, "Liberal Jews could and did claim that Jewish faith and practice were the result of historical development."

It is this idea of evolution that most defines the strength of the movement. When Adam and Eve lived in *Gan Eden*, they were given no choice: they were not to eat of a certain tree that would teach them more than human beings needed to know. When the first earthlings did indeed choose to disobey, they were punished.

Reform Judaism has an exalted, evolved image of human beings who are capable of choice. We've come a long way from the garden! Perhaps we've grown and so has God.

Free to Choose

Reform Jews may choose their rituals and beliefs, and the model applies to the rabbinate as well. Within the bounds of encouragement and discouragement, we are allowed to decide whether, for example, to celebrate one or two days of Rosh Hashanah [Jewish New Year], to keep *kashrut*, or to sanctify a same-sex marriage. Choice, however, depends upon knowing enough to practice the art of distinction. When the early reformers did away with traditional rituals such as *kashrut*, circumcision, and *Shabbat* [Sabbath] on Saturday, and with traditional beliefs such as the coming of a messiah, the restoration of the Temple and sacrifices, and angelology, [the study of the biblical doctrine of angels], they were experimenting with the ingredients necessary to maintain Jewish civilization, to use Kaplan's definition of Judaism. The title of Wise's *siddur* [prayer book], *Minhag America*, was a response to a new Jewish experience. In this prayer book, written in the holy language of Hebrew as well as English, we find a traditional order of service with all the seemingly archaic parts removed.

Jews often decide what is objectionable not only by their own compass but by the non-Jewish world. Since Exodus, when the people rose up against Moses by challenging him with what the world will think of a God who takes a people out of a country only to kill them in the desert, we have tried to give our neighbors nothing negative to say about us. Initially, the reformers articulated a Judaism more compatible with European Christians, at least aesthetically. Robes, organs, and sermons in the vernacular were a few innovations. Later, traditional, non-rational belief would be challenged.

My parents still had need for Judaism that was acceptable in the eyes of their co-religionists, yet my generation has been fortunate to live in a time that has allowed greater freedom of religious expression. We have been beneficiaries of little anti-semitism in America and we have different identity needs as Jews.

By the time of the Columbus Platform in 1937, with Nazism menacing, Reform Judaism characteristically shifted its doctrine to match the moment. The earlier Platform is suffused with universalism and rationalism; the word "Torah" does not appear. The Columbus Platform devotes a third of its document to religious practice and it speaks of a "providential God." The experiment begun in the 19th century was being modified, improving itself by being responsive to its followers. An eternal community, Israel may still live because of its great capacity to keep the big picture and to widen its path. Most Reform congregations today are more traditional and ethnic in orientation than were their counterparts a generation ago.

After the destruction of the Temple, the rabbis taught us how to find other paths to God. Prayer, study, and good deeds substituted for animal sacrifices. We have always been an evolving people, and the journey has taught us that change is the essence of life, because life is dynamic.

Now Reform Judaism once again recognizes the need to expand the vision of modern Judaism. When our great-great-grandparents threw their *tefillin* [leather boxes containing biblical passages] and prayer shawls away, they knew what they were doing. When I served my first Reform congregation, I saw that my *balebatim* [synagogue elder] didn't have a clue as to what to do with the neatly folded *tallitot* [prayer shawls] sitting next to the prayer books—they only had Friday night services.

The Future of Judaism

The answer to what to do with prayer shawls is where I see Reform Judaism moving. The newest Pittsburgh Platform [1999] has been praised both by Orthodox leaders as well as those who are more classically Reform. How amazing! Yet really what this is about is education. Our people cannot make intelligent choices in practice and belief if they don't know more of the tradition. Whether a congregant wears a *tallit* is less important than whether he or she learns its meaning and is invited to try it. Understanding the potential power of certain rituals depends upon a rabbinate willing to experiment with the many Jewish possibilities for transcendence and transformation in a time when so many are yearning for this.

The speed with which a movement responds is a mark of its strength. Fifteen years ago I entered the rabbinical program at HUC [Hebrew Union College] in Jerusalem. One student *davened* [prayed] with *tefillin* and a handful elected to learn how to *leyn Torah* [chant the Law]. While many of us questioned the photograph on the cover of the winter issue (1999) of *Reform Judaism* of the president of CCAR [Central Conference of American Rabbis] laying *tefillin*, nevertheless it offered a new choice for some within the movement. The wish for more ceremony, practice, and Jewish community has been heard by the leaders of the Reform movement. Temple Emmanuel is alive and well in Manhattan and so are the congregations of Rodef Sholom, Stephen Wise, both in New York, and Temple Emanuel in Beverly Hills. All represent the full circle of what Reform Judaism is offering Jews at the close of the millennium.

The future of Judaism will ultimately depend on how inclusive it can be, and how well it can transmit its tradition. As Reform Judaism continues to move in strengthening the education of its people and in maintaining its unique commitment to change when necessary, it will easily meet the challenge of fulfilling God's promise to Abraham and Sarah [to make their descendants as numerous as the stars].

Reform Judaism is essential for Jewish life and it is the movement that will best carry Judaism forward. By meeting people where they are, rather than where we think they should be, we make Judaism welcoming, compelling, and helpful to individuals navigating life's journey. In the tradition of Reform Judaism, its rabbis gather Jews to become a community who demonstrate their love of God by serving each other and the world God created. This movement of gradual and radical change that has been most responsive to a post-Holocaust, increasingly egalitarian, pluralistic world, is the one that I want to serve as a member of the Central Conference of American Rabbis.

The Future of Conservative Judaism

by Clifford E. Librach

Conservative Judaism inhabits the middle ground of Jewish denominations. Not as progressive as Reform Judaism nor as traditional as Orthodox Judaism, it promotes an evolutionary Judaism that meets the social and political challenges of the twenty-first century. Zacharias Frankel, head of the Jewish Theological Seminary in Breslau, Germany, in the mid-1800s, formulated the philosophy behind Conservative Judaism. He advocated observance of Jewish traditions, adherence to religious laws *(halacha)* but with modifications suited to current needs, and the scientific and historical study of Judaism. Frankel saw Judaism as a continually changing and growing religious way of life.

In the United States, Conservative Judaism attracted Jews who were put off by the Orthodox branch, for whom strict adherence to religious laws and rituals were of paramount importance, but were also unhappy with the liberal Reform movement's stress on rationalism and modernity at the expense of tradition. The Jewish Theological Seminary of America (JTS), founded in 1886, became the training ground for Conservative rabbis and a world center of Jewish scholarship.

The future of Conservative Judaism is the topic of

the following selection by Clifford E. Librach. A Reform rabbi, Librach argues that Conservative Judaism is becoming more liberal as was seen in the JTS's 1983 decision to ordain women. That decision caused a division in the Conservative movement and led to what Librach describes as a "continuous tilt and drift to the Left." In his view, Conservative Judaism may soon adopt some of the practices of the Reform branch, such as tolerance of intermarriage and the official embrace of homosexuality through the ordination of gays and lesbians as rabbis. In time, according to Librach, American Jewish congregations may completely move away from the idea of separate, distinctive denominations. This antiestablishment mood can already be seen in the changes taking place in the ordination of rabbis.

In any religion, the middle position is the hardest to define and the toughest to defend. For American Jews, this position has been occupied for close to a century by Conservative Judaism. Until very recently, indeed, most American Jews affiliated with synagogues have, in the tripartite [three-part], division of modern Judaism, found their home in this movement, a uniquely American phenomenon that locates itself between the "extremes" of Reform to its Left and Orthodoxy to its Right.

Since its inception in the late 19th century, Conservative Judaism has insisted that, unlike Reform, it is committed to Judaism not only as a faith but as a system of *law*, and to the norms of ritual behavior embodied in the rabbinic legal tradition known as *halakhah*. At the same time, and in contrast to Orthodoxy on its Right, Conservatism has also prided itself on its flexibility, its willingness to adapt to modern ideas. Examples of how this balancing act has worked itself out historically included these: while adhering formally to such staples of strict Jewish religious practice as the laws of diet (*kashrut*) and Sabbath-observance, the Conservative movement long ago ruled that mixed seating was permitted in religious services, as was driving to the synagogue on the Sabbath. More recently it has continued to mark its deviation from Orthodox norms by instituting complete egalitarianism between the sexes when it comes to leading public prayers and by ordaining women as rabbis.

A Movement in Trouble

But now the movement is in trouble. Just as American cultural life in general has become marked by the breakdown of consensus and the rise of polarization, so in Jewish religious life Conservatism has been finding the middle a lonely place. To the Left, Reform Judaism, demanding less and less of its adherents, offers an attractive and demographically bulging way-station for Conservative Jews on the road to religious oblivion. In the meantime, the still relatively small Orthodox movement, once perceived as hopelessly rigid and even bizarre in its unyielding attachment to the punctilious [careful] observance of religious law, is enjoying a surge of dynamism as a countercultural stay against the moral and spiritual anomie [social instability that stems from a lack of ideals] of postmodern America and non-Orthodox Judaism alike.

A good place to observe the tensions within today's Conservatism is the institution where, over the last century, the doctrinal arguments between tradition and the new have been conducted, where the resultant middle ground has been codified and promulgated, and where the movement's rabbis and cantors—its intermediaries with Conservative Jews "out there"—are trained. This is the Jewish Theological Seminary (JTS), Conservatism's rabbinical academy, located near Columbia University in New York City.

We are fortunate in having before us a new, two-volume history and self-analysis of the Seminary edited by Jack Wertheimer, a member of the JTS faculty and one of contemporary Judaism's premier sociologists and critics. To his great credit, Wertheimer has not attempted to offer in these two volumes a simple, linear account of the Seminary's history. Rather, he has invited a variety of perspectives from within and without the institution. The 36 separate essays in *Tradition Renewed* vary in style and quality, and there is more overlapping among them than one would like. But together they form a structure that amounts to more than its individual parts.

For the patient reader, there are many nuggets to be mined from these glimpses into a history rich in nuance, irony, high seriousness, and colorful personality. Coming as it does at a moment of ferment and crisis, *Tradition Renewed* offers a good occasion to reflect on the movement's past, present, and future.

Just as Conservative Judaism emerged on the American scene as a corrective to radical Reform, so JTS emerged as a corrective to Hebrew Union College (HUC), the training school in Cincinnati of Reform rabbis. The precipitating event can even be specified with precision. In 1883, at a celebration banquet for the first graduates of HUC, the Reform movement publicly proclaimed its liberation from tradional Judaism—"kitchen

Judaism," in the derisive phrase of Isaac Mayer Wise, Reform's founding father—by ostentatiously serving non-kosher delicacies to the assembled guests. The *"treifa* [any food forbidden by Jewish law] banquet," as it quickly became known, raised a storm of protest—several rabbis among the invited guests reportedly walked out—and sparked a search for another seminary to check HUC's then-monopoly in the field of non-Orthodox rabbinical education in America. . . .

The explicit mandate of this school was to offer regular rabbinic training in the English language, and to implement the methods and ideals of *Wissenschaft des Judentums*—literally, the scientific study of Judaism, an approach to the Jewish past pioneered in Germany by the 19th-century scholar Leopold Zunz. Religiously, this meant charting a course, to use the somewhat crude language of one of JTS's early supporters, "between stupid Orthodoxy and insane Reform."

Leaders of the Jewish Theological Seminary

To head the newly reorganized seminary and center of academic learning its benefactors recruited Solomon Schechter, the preeminent Jewish scholar in the English-speaking world. . . . As president, Schechter was to put the Seminary on the academic map. Over the course of his tenure he hired some of its greatest faculty members—including Louis Ginzberg, Alexander Marx, and Mordechai M. Kaplan—moved the school from a crowded downtown brownstone to more spacious quarters in Morningside Heights, and solidified JTS's long-term reputation for serious scholarship and rabbinic skill. . . . Schechter's chief obsession was "catholic Israel"—the eternal and universal community of the

Jews. Planting himself firmly in the middle, he sought to raise up a corps of rabbis who would in turn offer the swelling ranks of American Jewry a way to hold on to their familiar religious traditions without cutting themselves off from secular modernity.

Although he was the first and the most formative, Schechter was hardly the last in a gallery of brilliant figures who peopled JTS over the ensuing decades and turned it, faults and limitations notwithstanding, into a world center of Jewish learning. Pride of place on a long list should perhaps be given to two men: Saul Lieberman, an incomparable professor of Talmud who put his personal imprimatur [stamp of official approval] on rabbinic studies at JTS from 1940 until his death in 1983, and Louis D. Finkelstein, who became JTS president (later chancellor) in 1938 and served with distinction until his retirement in 1972. . . .

That Lieberman was a peerless scholar was a fact universally acknowledged at the Seminary, and the honor of studying with him was duly prized. But he was something less than a beloved figure. As generations of students and colleagues have testified, Lieberman was notoriously impatient when it came to almost any matter not directly involved with rabbinic scholarship, and he was also openly disdainful of congregational rabbis who were not themselves productive scholars (his term for them was "nurse-maids"). As the dominant faculty presence at JTS for 50 years, Lieberman was thus responsible for producing scores of Conservative rabbis who were intellectually overqualified and pyschologically demoralized, hardly a net boon either to scholarship or to their congregants.

Lieberman's privileged position at JTS was made possible politically by Louis Finkelstein, who protected him from many routine faculty responsibilities and nurtured both his scholarship and his ego. A solid scholar in his own right, Finkelstein was an especially gifted administrator—in the words of an essay by Michael B. Greenbaum in *Tradition Renewed*, "a shrewd and skilled politician who achieved much of what he set out to accomplish."

By the time of Finkelstein's retirement in 1972, his best years were long behind him and the Seminary had unfortunately fallen into sad shape. But during the decades when he was functioning at his peak, Finkelstein fostered an intellectual atmosphere that could permit the simultaneous presence at JTS of such disparate spirits as the ultra-rationalist Lieberman and the mystical-leaning Abraham Joshua Heschel. Finkelstein also had a passion for transmitting Jewish scholarship to the uneducated, Jewish and non-Jewish alike, and in his pursuit of that passion, through books and the various arts of public relations, he succeeded in making JTS and Conservative Judaism a real cultural presence in mid-century American religious life. . . .

A Fateful Decision

In 1983 the Seminary faculty voted to ordain women— a historic decision with substantial consequences for the future direction of the conservative movement. Indeed, if Reform's *treifa* banquet could be seen as the event that gave birth a century earlier to Conservatism's much more normative and traditionalist response to the challenge of modernity, the 1983 decision to ordain women, though hardly regarded that way at the time, may come to be perceived as marking a no less fateful reversal of course.

One immediate price paid for the decision was the disaffection of a number of key Seminary leaders and scholars, the most distiguished of whom was the talmudist [one who studies the Talmud, the body of Jewish law and lore] David Weiss-Halivni. Another faculty member opposed to the decision, David Novak, became active in an effort to establish a right-wing breakaway from Conservatism, complete with its own seminary and rabbinical association. Though this new movement, called the Union for Traditional Judaism, has never really taken off, the loss of these figures and others robbed JTS of the substantial weight of its own internal conservative ballast [a weight that balances a ship], causing what can only be described as a continuous tilt and drift to the Left over the last fifteen years.

Today, the most obvious symptom of this drift is the alliance that has been forged between the Conservative and Reform movements in this country to oppose state-sponsored Orthodoxy in Israel. This alliance obscures the very real doctrinal differences that still separate the two non-Orthodox movements, and to some concerned observers it has tainted the integrity of Conservatism by implicitly associating it with the more antinomian [freedom from rules and regulations] tendencies of Reform. They point in particular to Reform's unilateral decision to overthrow matrilineal descent [descent from the mother] as the sole determinant of an individual's Jewish identity; its apparent tolerance of intermarriage; its official embrace of homosexuality through the ordination of avowed gays and lesbians as rabbis; and its now widely anticipated designation of homosexual "marriages" as sanctified unions.

Despite these concerns, however, the bond between the two movements remains secure, and may actually be symptomatic of things to come. Many people now reasonably expect that, as was already the case with the ordination of women rabbis, JTS and the Conservative movement will eventually follow the path currently being blazed by Reform in a whole host of areas; all that will be required is the lag of a few years for decency's sake. . . .

Current Trends

May the time then come to think what is presently unthinkable? JTS is an institution in a search of an ideology, and the Conservative movement atop which it sits has reached a demographic plateau. Its population pool is spilling away, first into Reform, and from there into the moral vacuum of secular America. As for Reform, it has institutional problems of its own. HUC is now in the early phase of a reorganization. Financially the college is dependent upon a guaranteed percentage of congregational dues, but many congregations have begun to complain loudly about the burden, and the continued viability of HUC's four-campus structure (Cincinnati, New York, Los Angeles, and Jerusalem) may soon be in serious jeopardy.

Moreover, the landscape is now dotted with other institutions producing non-Orthodox rabbis for a Jewish public moving into a post-denominational phase. These include the Reconstructionist Rabbinical College in Philadelphia (the equivalent in rabbinic education of a school of osteopathic medicine) and the Academy for Jewish Religion in New York (the equivalent of an offshore medical school), both unable so far to achieve a status equal to that of JTS or HUC but each more than a blip on the screen. To these must also be added the phenomenon known as "private ordination," a practice taken from older models but long since abandoned for more highly structured forms of accreditation.

Today there are rabbis across the country who have been ordained by three other cooperating rabbis working with standards established by and for themselves. The usual justification for this procedure, as well as for the proliferation of non-"mainstream" seminaries, is that the mainstream schools are too narrow and authoritarian, and that their singular power needs to be checked by more "democratic" mechanisms. The anti-establishment mood is not a passing one, and may become more significant as increasing numbers of congregations, puzzled by what many already regard as mere peculiarities of outmoded doctrinal divisions, begin asking why institutional and "movement" affiliation should matter.

Reorganization and consolidation are facts of life in the corporate world. Such actions are either carefully planned or taken in the midst of panic and compulsion. As far as non-Orthodox American Jewish leaders are concerned, the challenge of the next century will be to arrest the course of atrophy and fragmentation that threatens to leave the center unguarded and ultimately empty. In the face of such drift, JTS and HUC may increasingly come to take on the aspect of dinosaurs, unable to adapt and hence slated for extinction.

Expressing a Jewish Identity: Current Trends

by G. Jeffrey MacDonald

In 1655 the Dutch West Indies Company allowed Jewish settlers to set up permanent residence in New Amsterdam, the future New York City. This event marked the beginning of a Jewish presence in the United States. After 350 years Judaism is firmly established in the fabric of American culture. Like all religious and cultural groups, young American Jews ask themselves what being Jewish means to them. After decades of assimilation during which their Jewish immigrant grandparents and great-grandparents melded into the larger, non-Jewish culture, young Jews today seek a greater identification with the culture and the faith of their forebears. They follow many different paths to the same goal: a sense of their heritage and identity.

"What Does 'Jewishness' Mean Today?" is the question posed in the following article from the *Christian Science Monitor*. In it, correspondent G. Jeffrey MacDonald examines social conditions and trends in Judaism through interviews with college students and academics. G. Jeffrey MacDonald is a freelance reporter who writes on religion. In 2002 he was named Templeton Reporter of the Year at the Religion Newswriters Association meeting in Nashville, Tennessee.

As a Jewish girl growing up in the 1980s and '90s in Greenwich, Conn., Alexis Gerber never struggled to fit into American society, as her ancestors did. Instead, she lived comfortably with her parents and two siblings in an upscale neighborhood where, she says, Jews were unwelcome some 60 years earlier.

Yet Ms. Gerber has nonetheless faced her own Jewish struggle, one that resonates with young Jews across the nation and is compelling Jewish institutions to raise tens of millions of dollars for the cause.

For many like Gerber, today's challenge is not for Jews to learn the ways of America, but rather for these Americans to learn how to live as Jews.

"I hated the rabbi. My mother hated the rabbi. So we never went" to synagogue, says Gerber, now a Tufts University senior with plans to become a rabbi herself. "It's not like I didn't have a Jewish identity. It was always very important. But I never did anything to express it."

As American Jewry turns 350 and looks to the future, Gerber's journey from disinterested to devotee tells of a new twist in a centuries-old story.

Rescue or Renaissance?

A people who perennially have struggled both to assimilate and also to maintain a cultural identity have by and large assimilated with flying colors. Jews currently live and work far beyond the Northeast urban enclaves of the previous centuries; 35 percent of the nation's 5.2 million Jews now live in the South and Midwest.

In a more controversial sign of blending, 47 percent of Jews who married after 1996 chose a non-Jewish spouse, up from 13 percent before 1970, according to the National Jewish Population Survey of 2000–2001.

With such thorough assimilation, however, has come the unprecedented task of "Judaizing" a bloc of ethnic Jews who can and sometimes do opt out of cultural Jewish life.

Whether the mega-project amounts to rescuing an endangered culture or fueling a vibrant renaissance depends on the vantage point of the speaker, but either way, Jews and their institutions are gearing up for what promises to be a new ballgame.

"Jews have made it," says Leonard Saxe, director of the Maurice and Marilyn Cohen Center for Modern Jewish Studies at Brandeis University in Waltham, Mass. "The issue now is not the fight against assimilation. It's giving the next generation of Jews a sense of their heritage and identity."

To that end, a surge of investment has swept the landscape of Jewish institutions:

• From 1960 to 1999, the number of non-Orthodox Jewish high schools jumped from 10 to 22. Since 2000, plans have taken shape for 13 more, some of which are already built.

• Between 1970 and 1999, the number of Jewish day schools affiliated with Reform Judaism grew from two to 22.

• The number of Chabad Lubavitch centers, which specialize in acquainting lapsed and secular Jews with the celebratory ways of Orthodox observance, has doubled from 300 in 1994 to about 600 in 2004.

• The budget for Hillel, the Jewish life centers with programs on more than 400 college and university campuses, has doubled from $25 million in 1994 to $52 million this year.

• More than 70,000 young Jewish adults have visited Israel in the past five years through Birthright Israel, a program that offers a free, 10-day trip to Jews ages 18 to 26.

All this investment speaks to a "mood of regeneration" in American Jewry at its 350th anniversary, according to Jack Wertheimer, provost and professor of American Jewish history at the Jewish Theological Seminary in New York.

Yet behind the shiny facade of new buildings sometimes lurks a fear that even a strict Jewish upbringing isn't enough to keep young people on the right path. This fear is represented in a decision by several Orthodox families to send their children who just graduated from high school to Israel for a year of yeshiva study, where students probe Hebrew Bible commentaries amassed through the centuries.

"The implication is striking," Dr. Wertheimer wrote in *The Jerusalem Post* in July. "Parents who are religiously observant and Jewishly engaged, who have sent their children to day schools from preschool through high school, raised them in dense Jewish communities, enrolled them in Jewish summer camps, and taken them on trips to Israel, seriously doubt whether they have adequately prepared their children to live as committed Jews in America's open society."

Ways of Being Jewish

Michael Vilarello knows the draw of that open society. Raised in Miami in the 1980s and '90s by a Jewish mother and Roman Catholic father who fled from Cuba as a child, he found his religious and ethnic identity were largely his to choose.

Yet he has chosen to regard himself as "100 percent Jewish," and to become active in Jewish life through Hillel at Middlebury College in Vermont, largely because he had attended Hebrew school three days a week as a child and studied two months at a Jewish high school in Israel.

Carrying on a Tradition

The following article from the Boston Globe *describes an ultra-Orthodox yeshiva outside of Boston where students prepare to become rabbis.*

It's morning and Getzel Merkowitz and Yossi Ginsborg, both 16, are about to begin their 16-hour school day. "Let's go," says Merkowitz, clutching a large Talmud which nearly fills the top of his wooden desk. He opens the oversized tome of Jewish law, and reads the first line in Hebrew, stroking his beard while rocking back and forth in meditation. He then translates the line into English in the same sing-song melody that Talmud students have used for centuries.

With 17 teenage boys and four rabbinical students filling the room, it's not quiet. But it's not supposed to be. Here, at the New England Hebrew Academy Yeshiva, they study Talmud and Torah out loud. . . . Through the years, the Hasidic yeshiva has turned out its share of distinguished graduates, including the chief rabbi of St. Petersburg, Menachem Mendel Pewzner. . . . Rabbi Moshe Lieberman, a soft-spoken, bearded 27-year-old man from Brooklyn, is the head of the yeshiva. He runs a tight ship, with lights out at 10:45 P.M., followed by a 6:45 A.M.

"I just didn't feel the same instant acceptance or click with the Latin American organization on campus," says Mr. Vilarello, now a senior at Middlebury.

Instead, for the first time in his life, he became a regular at Friday evening Shabbat services, because "it makes me feel at home. It's the prayers I learned every

wake-up call. He says it's all part of helping the future rabbis focus on scholarship and performing mitzvot (commandments or good deeds.) According to Lieberman, the emphasis on the Talmud is instrumental in helping students think in a logical way.

Despite the intense academics, the students do take breaks and have gotten to know the neighborhood. Thursday is their night out, when they head to Starbucks and then to the bowling alley. They also play pick-up basketball games a few times a week, and sing Hasidic melodies at fabrengens, or gatherings.

But in this old mansion, where English, Yiddish, and Hebrew are interchangeable, there's not much talk about missing the Internet or MTV. Just the experience of being away from home for the first time is enough to stir excitement among most of the students, say the lightly bearded youths. "We're as hip as they get," insists Merkowitz, who hopes to become a rabbi and have a family by the time he is 24. "We're teenagers. We do our studying and we talk about normal things, like the news and gossip; and then we go out to eat in the restaurant."

Steven Rosenberg, "It's Not Quiet Learning Talmud; After a Seven-Year Pause, a Hasidic Yeshiva Again Throws Open Its Doors," *Boston Globe*, March 3, 2002, p. 7.

day Thursday through Sunday from third grade through seventh grade. It feels right to be at these services."

Vilarello's passion for Jewishness has rubbed off.

In his first summer home from college, Vilarello's family adopted a new habit: lighting a candle at sundown every Friday to mark the Sabbath's arrival. Some friends have learned to like the Israeli music that now fills his iPod. And he considers it his job to invite Jews on campus to explore the riches of their tradition through Hillel.

For all its passion, however, Vilarello's approach highlights some of the challenges of the future in terms of claiming what it means to be a Jew in America.

The traditions, he says, are "presented to you in such a way that you can pick and choose what you want from being Jewish." For one person, therefore, living "Jewishly" might mean cooking traditional foods or collecting works by Jewish artists. For another, it might mean having Jewish friends or being active in progressive or pro-Israel politics.

Whether such a self-directed and individualistic approach can deliver a robust identity to American Jews remains to be seen.

Indeed, organizations committed to affirming Jewish "peoplehood" have struggled in recent years, according to Jonathan Sarna, chief historian of the anniversary project known as "Celebrate 350" and author of "American Judaism: A History."

B'nai B'rith, for instance, a primary magnet for Jewish donations and influence 100 years ago, now struggles to keep pace as donations flow to newer groups with more specialized missions.

"At a time when there are so many ways of being an American, it's not surprising there are many ways of being Jewish," Dr. Sarna says. "Yet what makes Jews distinct is that Jews are both a people and a religion. . . . You can't have one without the other."

Even the loosely knit movement known as Orthodox Judaism, whose participants define themselves by holding closely to Jewish law and custom, has in some sectors accepted that Jewish identity is up to the individual to define. For instance, not all members of the Orthodox Congregation Shearith Israel in New York City keep kosher [maintain strict dietary practices], according to Senior Rabbi Marc Angel, although the leadership there hopes someday they will.

"We have different people looking for different things," Mr. Angel says. "Still, we believe if people are exposed to Jewish law in a serious way, they will be attracted. . . . We hope they're moving closer to the tradition rather than away from it."

Going forward past the 350-year landmark, Jewish institutions entrusted with passing on traditions are facing pressure to review what makes them relevant in today's setting, where the dynamics and challenges have changed so dramatically from the days when Jews were barred from certain neighborhoods and industries.

Prominent Jewish philanthropist Michael Steinhardt, for instance, has publicly criticized some of American Jewry's historic groups for being "backward-seeking organizations," preoccupied with yesterday's problems. He has instead steered his considerable resources to new projects, such as Birthright Israel.

But in the view of Dr. Saxe, of Brandeis University, historic institutions may continue to play a vital role, especially if they can adapt to the changing needs and demands of the people they serve. "Jewish institutions, whatever they are, are going to have to figure out how to play different roles," he says.

The secular ones might have to infuse more religious content into their programming, he says, while the religiously conservative ones might need to accept such difficult realities as intermarriage.

"They'll need to provide opportunities for the next generation of Jews at least to know what this tradition is and choose if they want to be part of it," Saxe says. "You really can't reject something that you don't know. You can ignore it, but you can't reject it until you learn about it."

Support for Israel

by Dan Ephron

The Land of Israel (Eretz Yisrael) is one of the most important aspects of Judaism. Jews believe the Land of Israel, originally called Canaan, was promised by God to Abraham for his descendants. The ancient Israelites returned to this "promised land" after centuries of enslavement in Egypt and remained until their deportation by the Babylonians in 598 B.C. and again in 586 B.C. After seventy years of exile the Jews were permitted to return to the Land of Israel. For six hundred years they lived under Persian, Greek-Syrian, and Roman rulers while maintaining the freedom to run their day-to-day affairs. This situation ended in A.D. 70 when Rome crushed a Jewish revolt, destroyed the Temple in Jerusalem, and drove the Jews into exile. Despite the Diaspora (the name given to the dispersal of the Jews by their conquerors) small numbers of Jews remained in the renamed Palestine and migrated back during the following centuries. It was not until the late 1800s that a full-scale return to the Land of Israel was promulgated by the leaders of the Zionist movement. The Zionist goal of creating a national homeland for the Jewish people became a reality in 1948 with the founding of the state of Israel.

The three main branches of Judaism—Orthodox, Conservative, and Reform—support the state of Israel in either religious, cultural, or political contexts, or all three.

For some Jews Israel is a place of religious pilgrimage, some send donations of money for various causes, and some urge their political leaders to support the state of Israel on the world stage. And, finally, some Jews make the dramatic decision to move to Israel. The following selection by former *Boston Globe* reporter Dan Ephron deals with the issue of North American Jewish immigration to Israel. In recent years, as Ephron points out, North American Jews have helped Israel maintain its Jewish ethnicity by immigrating. Grants from the government of Israel help the newcomers settle in, but Ephron's interviewees maintain that there is more to their decision to immigrate than the financial aid.

Dan Ephron is currently a Jerusalem correspondent for *Newsweek* magazine.

Aaron Goldberg will train dogs for the Israeli police. David Gross hopes to find work as a baker. And Amos Ben Harav plans to study mechanical engineering.

The three men were among a planeload of Jews who arrived at Ben-Gurion Airport yesterday [July 14, 2004] from the United States and Canada as new immigrants, ushered to Israel by a private group that has significantly boosted immigration by North American Jews over the past three years, even as violence has surged.

The group, Nefesh B'Nefesh (Jewish Souls United), has helped persuade 1,500 American Jews this summer alone to sell their belongings, uproot their families, and begin new lives in Israel.

Although that number represents only a fraction of the overall migration to Israel, it highlights an interesting trend. While immigration from other countries has

dropped by half since the start of the Palestinian upris-
ing in the West Bank and Gaza Strip in 2000, American
Jews keep coming.

"When Israel appears to be in some kind of danger,
the trend is that immigration to Israel from the US goes
up," said Howie Kahn, a counselor for the Association
of Americans and Canadians in Israel, which helps immigrants adjust to the Jewish state.

"There's a little craziness to immigrating. Your family is happy, your kids are in their schools, and sud-
denly you go to a place where you might not even have
a job. It's not necessarily a logical decision, so to look
for logic isn't the right approach," he said.

While other countries turn away newcomers, Israel
has always encouraged Jewish immigration.

Sending a Message

In a country surrounded by hostile neighbors and ob-
sessed with demographics, *aliyah* (literally "ascension")
is widely perceived here as the Zionist counterweight to
the high Arab birthrate in Israel.

Incentives offered to immigrants over the years have
included free flights to Israel, tax breaks, and lower interest on state-sponsored mortgage loans. Incentives have
been reduced slightly in recent years for budget reasons.

The policy has helped Israel keep its Jew-to-Arab ratio
more or less constant since the 1950s at about 4-1. And
while most immigrants arrived from regions of economic or political hardship—Jews from Arab countries
in the 1950s and '60s, the Soviet Union in the 1970s,
and Russia in the 1990s—some waves have boosted Israel's economic output.

"By coming here, you have sent a strong message to

the world that Israel is and always will be the eternal homeland of the Jewish people," Prime Minister Ariel Sharon said at an airport hangar yesterday morning, during a 90-minute ceremony for the 400 new Israelis after their 12-hour flight from New York.

Israeli folk songs from the 1950s were played over a loudspeaker and a clown twisted balloons in the shape of animals for children.

But while immigrants from North America over the years included a few famous figures, former prime minister Golda Meir and the Arab-hating Rabbi Meir Kahane, for example, they never amounted to more than a couple of thousand a year. About 140,000 North Americans now live in Israel.

Immigration officials say the annual number averaged about 1,500 until Nefesh B'Nefesh was founded three years ago by two American Jews to promote *aliyah*. It jumped to 2,000 in 2002 and 2,500 the next year. Organizers hope to reach 3,000 this year.

Part of the draw is the roughly $20,000 loan Nefesh B'Nefesh gives each family to help defray the cost of starting over in a new country. Nearly all of that financing comes from private philanthropic sources in the United States.

The group also handles much of the immigration bureaucracy for the families, which in Israel can be grueling.

But organizers say the main reason for their success is their ability to market Israel as a place with spiritual meaning, especially for observant Jews, who made up an estimated 80 percent of the immigrants yesterday.

In the past, secular Jews accounted for a greater proportion of immigrants from the United States.

Kahn said of the immigration initiative: "They are

selling aliyah in various communities like you would sell a product. They use PR [public relations] people, they have wonderful advertising."

Some immigrants said they were frustrated with American life. Kimberley Juroviesky, from Boca Raton, Fla., who was holding her 1-month-old baby, Azaria, was heading for a kibbutz to live communally with other Israelis. She said, "We are looking for a better life for our children. We found Americans too materialistic. They are only looking out for themselves. They live life to work and buy things."

None said they were deterred by the violence.

"No amount of terrorism, no amount of economic hardship will stop these immigrants from calling Israel their home," one of the two Nefesh B'Nefesh founders, Tony Gelbart, told the cheering crowd. Aaron Goldberg, who arrived yesterday, would certainly agree. Though he had been to Israel only once before, Goldberg said he had talked to his wife about moving to Israel since they married 15 years ago.

Wearing a tzitzit under his shirt (a fringed garment worn by religious Jews) Goldberg described quitting his job as a dog trainer in Hollywood, Fla., and packing the belongings of his wife and four children in a clutch of suitcases.

"It's quite traumatic, but I feel in my heart that it's the right move," he said at the airport. Goldberg will live in the town of Rehovot, south of Tel Aviv, where he's been offered a job training Israeli police dogs.

Amos Ben Harav was among the younger immigrants on the plane. A 19-year-old Boston University student, Ben Harav is transferring to the Technion, Israel's prestigious technical college, to complete his degree in mechanical engineering.

Born in Israel, Ben Harav left the country with his parents and moved to Boston before his second birthday. "They moved away from here, but they're proud that I'm moving back," he said. His older brother, who immigrated a year ago and now serves in the Israeli army, showed up at the airport to greet him.

Nefesh B'Nefesh says 99 percent of the Jews it has brought to Israel in the past three years have remained here. If true, the program is a raging success. The attrition rate for North American Jews since Israel's founding in 1948 surpasses 30 percent, according to Kahn.

But Kahn says the true test for Nefesh B'Nefesh participants will come three years after their arrival, when the $20,000 loan becomes a grant and the immigrants are free to return to the United States without having to pay it back.

"Most immigrants who go back tend to do so not necessarily in the first year or two but rather in the first five years," he said.

For David Gross, who emigrated from Toronto, the idea of returning seems improbable. "We sold a business, a home, and two cars," said Gross, who owned a restaurant and later worked as a baker. "I think it's safe to say we'll be here for a long time."

Glossary

ark: A cupboard or chest at the front of the sanctuary in the synagogue where Torah scrolls are kept.

bar mitzvah: The religous coming-of-age of a boy—at age thirteen the boy is expected to observe the commandments; also the religious ceremony marking this event.

bat mitzvah: The religious coming-of-age of a girl—at age twelve the girl is expected to observe the commandments; also the ceremony marking this event.

Canaan: The land in the Middle East inhabited by Abraham and his descendants and to which the Israelites returned when Moses led them out of slavery.

commandment: Any religious duty or obligation; according to the Jewish tradition there are 613 commandments referred to in the Torah.

Conservative: A denomination of Judaism that allows modifications in Jewish religious law but which retains some traditional rituals and customs.

diaspora: A word used to describe the Jewish communities outside of Israel; also refers to the dispersal of the Jews after the Babylonian Exile in 586 B.C. and Roman destruction of Jerusalem and the Second Temple in A.D. 70.

Exodus: The book of the Bible that describes the Israelites' departure from Egypt.

First Temple: The house of worship built by Solomon in Jerusalem around 950 B.C. and destroyed by the Babylonians in 586 B.C.

Gemara: Rabbinic commentary on Mishnah and the decisions reached during these discussions; incorporated into the Talmud.

Haggadah: The book from which the traditional narrative is recited at the Passover seder.

halacha: Jewish religious law, custom, practice, or ritual. Anything called "halachic" is regarded as proper behavior.

Hanukkah: Festival recalling the victory of the Maccabees over their Greek-Syrian rulers.

Hasidism: A ultrapious Orthodox sect of Judaism founded in Eastern Europe in the 1700s; followers are known as Hasids.

Haskalah: The Jewish Enlightenment movement advocating Jewish participation in modern European society and pursuit of secular education.

High Holidays: Rosh Hashanah (the Jewish New Year) and Yom Kippur (the Day of Atonement).

kosher: A Hebrew word meaning "fit" or "proper"; anything that meets Jewish dietary laws.

Magen David: "Shield of David"; the six-pointed star which is a symbol of Judaism; it is also part of the blue and white flag of the state of Israel.

matzo: Unleavened bread; an important part of the Passover seder.

menorah: The seven- or nine-branched candelabrum that is an important symbol in Judaism.

midrash: From the Hebrew word *drash*, meaning "to inquire"; the body of complete commentary on Scripture.

minyan: A prayer quorum of ten adult males.

Mishnah: A Hebrew word meaning "teaching"; the codification of the Oral Law achieved by Rabbi Judah Ha-Nasi.

mitzvah: Religious commandment; also applies to a good deed.

Oral Law: Corpus of rulings and instructions handed down by God to Moses at Sinai and passed on by word of mouth from generation to generation.

Orthodox: The denomination of Judaism that is most traditional and strict in adhering to religious law and practice.

rabbi: The qualified teacher of Judaism and the spiritual leader of a congregation.

Reconstructionism: A movement founded by Mordecai Kaplan that regards Judaism as a civilization and an evolving culture that continually adapts to the world around it.

Reform: A denomination of Judaism that departs from many traditional religious laws and rituals and advocates adaptation to the demands of modern society.

Rosh Hashanah: Jewish New Year.

Sabbath: *Shabbat* in Hebrew; the seventh day of the week; the day dedicated to rest and to God. Sabbath begins at sundown on Friday evening and ends at sundown the following evening.

Second Temple period: In ancient times, the era from the rebuilding of the Temple in 520 B.C. to its destruction by the Romans in A.D. 70.

seder: The home service and meal that takes place on the first two nights of Passover.

Septuagint: First Greek translation of the Bible.

Shema: Jewish statement of belief beginning with the words "Hear, O Israel."

shofar: Ram's horn blown on Rosh Hashanah and on other occasions.

siddur: Prayer book.

tallith (or tallis): Prayer shawl worn by Jewish males during prayer services.

Talmud: The codification of Jewish lore, composed of the Mishnah and the Gemara.

Torah: The Five Books of Moses; more generally, Jewish religious teachings.

yeshiva: A Jewish academy of higher learning where students prepare to become rabbis.

Yom Kippur: Day of Atonement; a day of fasting and prayer in which Jews reflect on their failings, remember their departed loved ones, and pray for redemption.

Chronology

ca. 3000 B.C.
Human settlements appear in Asia Minor, Mesopotamia, and Egypt.

ca. 2500
The Egyptian pharoahs build the Great Pyramids in Egypt.

ca. 2000–1700
Abraham is born in southern Mesopotamia and later moves his family to the land of Canaan. During a famine his grandson Jacob moves his family to Egypt.

ca. 1280
Moses leads the Israelites out of Egypt where they had been enslaved. While in Sinai, he receives the Torah from God for the Israelites.

ca. 1250–1050
The Israelites conquer Canaan, settle the land, and divide it among twelve tribes.

ca. 1020–1004
Saul is chosen as the first king of Israel.

ca. 1004–965
David, Saul's successor, rules a united kingdom of Israel and enlarges it.

ca. 965-922
Solomon, son of David, rules Israel and builds the First Temple in Jerusalem.

ca. 922
Upon Solomon's death, his kingdom is divided into two domains: Israel in the north and Judah in the south.

722
Assyria conquers the kingdom of Israel; the northern tribes of Israel are exiled.

612
The Assyrians are conquered by the Babylonians.

586
Babylonian king Nebuchadrezzar II conquers the kingdom of Judah, destroys Jerusalem and the First Temple, and exiles the people to Babylon.

539
The Persians conquer Babylon; Persian king Cyrus II allows Judeans to return to their land, but many decide to remain in Babylon.

515
The construction of the Second Temple is completed.

332
Following the conquest of the Persian Empire and Israel by Alexander the Great, Hellenistic culture is introduced in Israel.

167
Antiochus IV Epiphanes, the Seleucid king of Syria, profanes the Temple in Jerusalem and forces the Israelites to accept Hellenistic culture.

165

The Maccabees lead a successful Jewish revolt against the Seleucids. Judah is an independent state until 63 B.C.

63

Rome expands its power in the eastern Mediterranean and annexes Judea.

37

Herod is appointed king of Judea by the Romans and sets about renovating the Second Temple.

A.D. 30

Jesus of Nazareth is crucified.

66

Jewish revolt against Roman rule begins.

70

Romans destroy Jerusalem and the Second Temple, crushing the Jewish revolt and forcing the Jews into exile.

200

The Mishnah, a compilation of the Oral Law, legal debates, and discussions concerning all facets of Jewish life, is collated and edited by Rabbi Judah Ha-Nasi.

219–259

Babylon emerges as a center of Jewish life and learning.

313

First legal restrictions on Jews follows the legalization of Christianity in the Roman Empire.

400

Jerusalem Talmud is completed. The Talmud is the interpretation and elaboration of the Mishnah.

476

Fall of the Roman Empire in the West; Babylonian Talmud is completed. This is the ultimate compilation of the Oral Law.

612

Muhammad, the founder of Islam, begins his career as a prophet on the Arabian Peninsula.

638

Muslims conquer Israel and allow Jews to return to Jerusalem.

715

With Muslim conquest of northern Africa (700–705) and Spain (711–713), Jewish settlements spread throughout the western Mediterranean.

900

Jews experience widespread religious toleration in the Muslim world and flourish on the Iberian Peninsula. They are traders, merchants, doctors, poets, and philosophers.

1096

During the First Crusade, Jews of the Rhineland area of northern France and Germany are massacred by followers of the crusade.

1204

Moses Maimonides, Jewish philosopher, physician, and codifier of Jewish law, dies.

1391
Spanish Jews are persecuted and forced to convert to Christianity.

1492
Jews are expelled from Spain at the instigation of the Spanish Inquisition.

1497
Jews are expelled from Portugal.

1500
With the rise of the Ottoman Empire, Jewish communities within the empire experience religious freedom and economic opportunity.

1516
Jews in the city-state of Venice are forced to live in ghettos, walled-off sections of the city.

1654
First Jewish immigrants arrive in New Amsterdam (now New York City) seeking religious freedom.

1730
First synagogue in North America, Congregation Shearith Israel in New York City, is dedicated.

1760
Hasidism, an ultrapious sect of Judaism noted for its ecstatic worship and group cohesion, is established by Israel ben Eliezer, known as Ba'al Shem Tov.

1770
Haskalah, the Jewish Enlightenment, begins. The movement

advocates Jewish participation in German society and leads to social and educational reforms.

1786
Moses Mendelssohn, philosopher of the Jewish Enlightenment, dies.

1820
Reform movement begins in Germany. Reform Judaism does away with many practices and beliefs of Orthodox Judaism.

1830
Beginning of large German-Jewish immigration to the United States.

1881
Beginning of large Eastern European Jewish immigration to the United States.

1885
In the Pittsburgh Platform, Reform leaders stand for progressivism and reject Jewish religious law (halacha) as binding on Jews.

1886
The Conservative movement establishes its own rabbinical school, the Jewish Theological Seminary, in New York City.

1896
Theodor Herzl calls for the return of Jews to Israel and initiates the movement of political Zionism.

1917
Following the end of World War I the British declare their support for a Jewish homeland in Palestine, formerly part of the Ottoman Empire.

1922

Reconstructionist movement of Judaism is established by Mordecai Kaplan.

1935

In Nazi Germany the Nuremberg Laws revoke the rights of German Jews on the basis of race.

1938

Nazis destroy Jewish property and synagogues in Germany and Austria.

1940

Nazis force Jews into ghettos and seize their property.

1941–1945

Approximately 6 million Jews are murdered outright or worked to death in Nazi concentration camps.

1948

The state of Israel is established.

1950

The state of Israel declares that every Jew has the right to settle in Israel (the Law of Return).

1967

Jewish Reconstructionist movement admits women to its rabbinical program.

1972

Reform movement ordains the first woman rabbi.

1983

On the issue of "Who is a Jew?" the Reform movement recognizes as Jewish the children of marriages between a male Jew and a female non-Jew in cases in which the children are raised in Judaism.

2000

Approximately 5.8 million Jews live in the United States, composing 2 percent of the population.

For Further Research

Books

Robert Alter, *The Five Books of Moses: A Translation with Commentary.* New York: W.W. Norton, 2004.

Bernhard W. Anderson, *Understanding the Old Testament.* Englewood Cliffs, NJ: Prentice-Hall, 1986.

David S. Ariel, *What Do Jews Believe? The Spiritual Foundations of Judaism.* New York: Schocken, 1995.

Philip Birnbaum, *A Book of Jewish Concepts.* New York: Hebrew Publishing Company, 1964.

Linda Burghardt, *The Bar and Bat Mitzvah Book.* New York: Citadel, 2004.

Norman F. Cantor, *The Sacred Chain: The History of the Jews.* New York: HarperCollins, 1994.

Joan Comay, *The Diaspora Story: The Epic Story of the Jewish People Among the Nations.* New York: Random House, 1980.

Alan M. Dershowitz, *The Vanishing American Jew: In Search of Jewish Identity for the Next Century.* Boston: Little, Brown, 1997.

Hayim Halevy Donin, *To Be a Jew: A Guide to Jewish Observance in Contemporary Life.* New York: BasicBooks, 1972.

Abba Eban, *Heritage: Civilization and the Jews.* New York: Summit, 1984.

Louis Finkelstein, ed., *The Jews: Their Role in Civilization.* New York: Schocken, 1971.

Samuel G. Freedman, *Jew vs. Jew: The Struggle for the Soul of American Jewry.* New York: Simon & Schuster, 2000.

Harry Gersh, *The Sacred Books of the Jews.* New York: Stein and Day, 1968.

Reuven Hammer, *Entering Jewish Prayer: A Guide to Personal Devotion and the Worship Service.* New York: Schocken, 1994.

Reuven Hammer, ed., *The Jerusalem Anthology: A Literary Guide.* Philadelphia: Jewish Publication Society, 1995.

J.H. Hertz, ed., *The Pentateuch and Haftorahs: Hebrew Text, English Translation and Commentary.* London: Soncino, 1976.

Barry W. Holtz, ed., *Back to the Sources: Reading the Classic Jewish Texts.* New York: Summit, 1984.

Jewish Publication Society, *Tanakh: A New Translation of the Holy Scriptures According to the Traditional Hebrew Text.* Philadelphia: Jewish Publication Society, 1985.

Steven T. Katz, *Jewish Philosophers.* New York: Bloch, 1975.

Francine Klagsbrun, *The Fourth Commandment: Remember the Sabbath Day.* New York: Harmony, 2002.

Isaac Klein, *A Guide to Jewish Religious Practice.* New York: Jewish Theological Seminary of America, 1979.

Jacob Neusner, *Judaism: An Introduction.* New York: Penguin, 2002.

F.E. Peters, *Children of Abraham: Judaism, Christianity, Islam.* Princeton, NJ: Princeton University Press, 1982.

Rabbinical Assembly, United Synagogue of Conservative Judaism, *Etz Hayim: Torah and Commentary.* Philadelphia: Jewish Publication Society, 2001.

Chaim Raphael, *Festival Days: A History of Jewish Celebrations.* New York: Grove Weidenfeld, 1991.

George Robinson, *Essential Judaism: A Complete Guide to Beliefs, Customs, and Rituals.* New York: Pocket Books, 2000.

Norman Roth, ed., *Medieval Jewish Civilization: An Encyclopedia.* New York: Routledge, 2003.

Jonathan Sarna, *American Judaism: A History.* New Haven, CT: Yale University, 2004.

Milton Steinberg, *Basic Judaism.* New York: Harcourt Brace, 1975.

Ira Steingroot, *Keeping Passover: Everything You Need to Know to Bring the Ancient Tradition to Life and Create Your Own Passover Celebration.* San Francisco: HarperSanFrancisco, 1995.

Adin Steinsaltz, *The Essential Talmud.* New York: BasicBooks, 1976.

Daniel B. Syme, *The Jewish Home: A Guide for Jewish Living.* Northvale, NJ: Jason Aronson, 1989.

Geoffrey Wigoder, ed., *The New Encyclopedia of Judaism.* New York: New York University Press, 2002.

Web Sites

American Jewish Historical Society, www.ajhs.org. This site fosters awareness and appreciation of the American Jewish heritage. It has extensive research collections relating to American Jewish history.

Gemara (Talmud), www.acs.ucalgary....al/TalmudMap/Gemara.html. This academic site provides a sample of the standard printed Talmud page and extensive descriptions of all of its elements.

The Hebrews, a Learning Module, www.wsu.edu.8080~dee/HEBREWS/HEBREWS.htm. This Web site from Washington State University provides an overview of the history of the ancient Hebrews from the era of the Patriarchs to the Roman conquest of Jerusalem.

Internet Jewish History Sourcebook, www.fordham.edu/hals all/jewish/jewishbook.html. An academic site with numerous primary sources and links to other sites.

The Jewish Museum, www.jewishmuseum.org. The Web site of the New York City museum that houses a collection of over twenty-eight thousand objects of different media, including ceremonial art.

Jewish Virtual Library, a Division of the American-Israeli Cooperative Enterprise, www.jewishvirtuallibrary.org. An online encyclopedia of Jewish history and culture, this site contains Judaic treasures of the Library of Congress.

My Jewish Learning, www.myjewishlearning.com. A transdenominational Web site of Jewish education and information, My Jewish Learning is geared toward learners of all ages and educational backgrounds.

Navigating the Bible, www.bible.ort.org. Prepared by ORT, the Jewish international charity whose focus is on education and training, this site serves as an online bar/bat mitzvah tutor. Among other things, readers can study the Five Books of Moses with commentaries, read weekly Torah readings, and learn to sing the Torah notes.

Videos

Hasidism: A Life Apart, directed by Menachem Daum and Oren Rudavsky, First Run Features, 1997. A film exploring the way of life of the Jews known as Hasidim, whose distinctive way of life sets them apart from the mainstream American culture. Available in VHS format.

Heritage: Civilization and the Jews, 1984. A nine-episode PBS series that focuses on the history of the Jews and their contributions to world civilization. Available in DVD or VHS formats.

Index